Irina The Killer

Ana Benton

Published by Trellis Publishing, 2021.

While every precaution has been taken in the preparation of this book, the publisher assumes no responsibility for errors or omissions, or for damages resulting from the use of the information contained herein.

IRINA THE KILLER

First edition. July 10, 2021.

Copyright © 2021 Ana Benton.

ISBN: 979-8224313273

Written by Ana Benton.

IRINA THE KILLER

ANA BENTON

1

Female serial killers are incredibly rare because the women, in general, are not prone to murdering more than one person. Even if they do, they usually use poison or kill their victims in a non-violent way. Brutality is not common, and it is more prominent when the authorities are dealing with a male killer. However, Irina Viktorovna Gaidamachuk does not match the standard description of a serial murderer. She didn't kill because she thought it was fun or felt an urge to take someone's life. Instead, Irina did it because she needed money to feed her ever-growing alcohol addiction which did fit into the profile because she killed in order to gain wealth.

The addiction ruined her life and left her penniless at the beginning of the 2000s. Therefore, she saw only one solution – stealing. Often, her thefts included a tragic end for a person who was being robbed. Irina didn't want to leave any witnesses behind. But she was eventually caught and apprehended by the Russian authorities. Irina became known as Raskolnikov in a skirt, Satan in a skirt, She-wolf of Krasnoufimsk, and Maniac-woman from Sverdlovsk in the Russian media which covered this case extensively. Her trial was an absolute sensation because nobody could believe she eluded the police for so long. Not to forget that Russia didn't have a female serial killer in a very long time.

Early life

Irina Viktorovna Gaidamachuk was born on September 26th, 1972 in a small town called Nyagan, Khanty–Mansi Autonomous Okrug. It is located in the central part of the Soviet Union, or present-day Russia. Irina Gaidamachuk belonged to the working class, and both of her parents had low paying jobs at the time. Unsatisfied with their financial situation, Irina's parents spent all of their money on alcohol. Irina grew up with two addicts in the household so it should come as no surprise to find out she started consuming alcohol at a very young age. The girl didn't think twice about it because she found that behavior completely normal. After all, the people who took care of her did the same. She soon became addicted and would drink alcohol on a daily basis.

The relatives and neighbors who knew the Gaidamachuk family noticed that Irina was regularly intoxicated and it was concerning. The authorities were notified, and child protection services took Irina away from her parents in hopes of stopping her self-destructive behavior. She lived in a foster home, but once she turned eighteen, she was forced to move out and take care of herself. Irina left Nyagan and moved to Krasnoufimsk, Sverdlovsk Oblast at the beginning of the 1990s hoping she could start her life over in a new location. And she was partially right because she met her future husband Yuri in Krasnoufimsk. The two fell in love instantly and started a family. Yuri ignored Irina's obvious addiction hoping it is not too severe. As a matter of fact, she was able to hide it pretty well at first, especially during the pregnancies.

Irina's family was expanding rapidly, and she gave birth to two children during the 1990s. However, as the decade came to the end, she started drinking more and more, neglecting her family. Yuri knew that giving Irina money would surely result in a new bottle of alcohol even though she would promise that she will buy food and groceries. She was unemployed because of the fact that she was constantly intoxicated. Nobody wanted to have her as an employee because Irina was irresponsible and would sometimes steal money from the establishment she worked at in order to buy liquor. Without ideas or options, Irina came up with a plan to start attacking and robbing the elderly women that lived in the area. She figured they would be easy to scare and get them to give up all of their money.

The beginning of the killing spree

It was the year 2002 when Irina Viktorovna Gaidamachuk began to put her plan into the motion. She figured out it would be best to pretend to be a social worker because she needed to gain access to the apartments of the elderly women without causing a commotion. Knowing the situation in the country itself, Irina was confident that the women would believe a figure of authority and that they would welcome her into their home. Since she needed the money as soon as possible, Irina started looking around her neighborhood for potential victims. Krasnoufimsk had a large population of the elderly women and Irina knew that she could easily find someone to rob. But one thought crept into her mind – what if the women could recognize her after the crime was committed? That's when she decided it would be better to kill the victim right away, and then take their money.

The first murder went better than she expected. The elderly woman living in Krasnoufimsk opened her door and let Irina in. She was well-dressed and polite, so it was impossible not to buy her story. Once Irina established that the woman was home alone, she didn't waste any time and immediately started hitting her with an axe. The crime was brutal, and the woman was left lying in a pool of blood with deep cuts on her upper body, including the head. But unfortunately for Irina, the woman didn't have plenty of money. The amount was quite low, and Irina didn't get to buy enough alcohol to last her for more than a week. Disappointed by the first try but determined to do better next time, Irina drank the alcohol, forgetting what she did in order to buy it. At the same time, the police discovered the body of a murdered elderly woman and they were shocked by the sight. The murder scene was gruesome, and they suspected the perpetrator was surely a man.

After all, they had seen plenty of similar acts committed by males and the thought that a woman was somehow involved didn't even cross their minds. Irina was confident that her plan was great, so she moved on to find more victims. In the next couple of years, she added a hammer as one of her murder weapons and would bludgeon elderly women to death before robbing their homes. She knew how to clean up afterward so there would be no physical evidence left at the crime scene. Irina also tried burning a couple of houses down in order to cover her tracks. She made the arson look like an accident, so the police had some issues with establishing if the fire was intentional or not. Luckily, the fires were put out before they managed to spread, so there were no additional victims. Growing more and more confident, Irina started killing in other surrounding cities such as Yekaterinburg, Serov, Achit, and Druzhinino. But the majority of the crimes were committed in the place she actually lived in with her family.

The police investigation

Realizing that something serious was happening in the Sverdlovsk Oblast because at least six elderly women were found dead, massacred and robbed in their homes, the local law enforcement started connecting these cases and suspecting they were somehow linked. This happened in 2005, so Irina was killing for three years without being on a police radar. Since they suspected only one person is behind all these murders, the police started interviewing the families and friends in hopes someone had seen or heard something prior to the killings. They were focused on finding a man and not a woman. After the crime scene analysis, the law enforcement was convinced that only a man would have enough power and strength to crush the skulls with a hammer or an axe.

However, one witness told the investigators that they saw a woman exiting a victim's apartment. This once again derailed the investigation because now the detectives were sure that the killer is using a disguise. Apparently, the killer was hiding their identity by wearing a wig and putting on women clothes. This actually sounded plausible to the investigators because it was an excellent way of avoiding being recognized on the street or looking suspicious to the neighbors. Russian Investigative Committee which got involved as soon as the official inquiry started speaking publicly about the case to the media.

When asked about the killer, they told the following: *"We believed at first that only a man could be so cruel as to slaughter in this way."*

The investigation actually lasted for years without reaching even a small breakthrough. The families of the victims were left in the dark, but that was common for that part of Europe because most of the police work is done behind the closed doors. The authorities were aware they had a serial killer on their hands and that they are still out there. Whoever it was, they were looking for unsuspecting victims, taking their money and killing them. Even though police dedicated plenty of their time to speak with the people linked to the cases, there were no new clues. However, they managed to connect a couple of crimes committed in the nearby cities to the same perpetrator because of the obvious similarities.

The female killer

Aware of the police investigation, Irina Viktorovna Gaidamachuk didn't feel an ounce of panic. As a matter of fact, she was certain that the law enforcement will never get to her, mostly because they were following the wrong trail by hunting a man and not a woman. She continued to kill and rob regardless of the fact that almost every woman she attacked had little to no money in their homes at the time of the murder. This didn't faze Irina much because she still managed to finance her alcohol addiction and buy the liquor she needed in order to feel alright. But just like every serial killer out there, Irina though that she was invincible and that was the first step to her downfall.

Russian authorities did deal with a couple of gruesome serial killers in the past, namely Sergey Golovkin who targeted young boys and Andrei Chikatilo who was a sadistic sex obsessed killer. So they knew the repercussions of having someone that dangerous roam the streets. Irina thought that nothing could happen to her and she became sloppy. She selected her victims carefully in the past, avoiding parts of the city she often visited and finding the woman that had no connection to her or her family. She still lived with her husband and children, pretending to be a decent mother with a small alcohol problem. Irina was still friendly with everyone she met and people found her to be shy. She made a first major mistake in 2010 when she selected another elderly woman called Bilbinur Makshaeva to be her new target. However, the woman was surprisingly strong, and she managed to avoid Irina's attack.

As a matter of fact, Irina's potential victim ran out of the apartment, screaming for help while Irina stood inside confused and shocked. Afraid that she might be identified, she picked up the money she could find at that moment and left the woman's apartment. Irina's victim was taken straight to the police station by her concerned neighbors, and she told the story of a woman entering her apartment and trying to kill her with a hammer. The police were shocked a bit at first because they recognized the modus operandi but the part that described the attacker as a woman made them think that the victim was so scared she didn't see the attacker properly. The elderly woman told the detectives that she was completely certain that a female entered her home by telling her she was a social worker.

This made the detectives wonder if they had the whole case wrong from the very beginning. They were starting to feel the urgency because they just realized they hunted the wrong person for more than five years. Bilbinur Makshaeva was still terrified by the experience, but she was able to describe her attacker and the police had the first sketch of the killer. Shocked by this discovery, the investigators started going through their old files, hoping a lead might come up but there was nothing they could work with. Russian Investigative Committee felt the urge to solve these crimes as soon as possible because the public was getting ruthless with the criticism. The case was dragging along and everyone thought that the law enforcement was incapable of solving such a serious crime. The citizens demanded that someone should be held responsible for the killings of the innocent and constantly talked about the fact that the police was not doing a great job since they missed a large part of the investigation.

Feeling the pressure, the Russian Investigative Committee arrested a woman they thought might be involved in the crimes. After all, they knew that the killer was female so they picked up a woman called Marina Valeeva who somewhat fit the description given by the victim who managed to escape. Marina didn't match the sketch entirely, but the police thought that she tried to change her appearance to avoid recognition. This case is a proof that false confessions happen everywhere because Marina was questioned for days and she eventually broke down confessing to sixteen murders. It will soon be discovered that Marina Valeeva was pressured by the police and kept awake for days in order to get her to admit that she was the perpetrator. The woman was found to be innocent because she couldn't describe any of the crimes accurately. Not to forget that she had the alibi for several murders because she was not in the area.

The last attack

Thinking that she might get away with it, Irina decided to attack a woman who lived near her family. It is still unclear why she choose to find someone she knew and murder them, especially while the police investigation was still ongoing. Surely, a person who had absolutely nothing to do with the murders was in custody at the time, but it is evident that Irina was overly confident in her abilities. Or she simply needed the money as soon as possible and didn't even think about the possibility of being identified. Battling an addiction is hard enough and the fact that she was actually killing people in order to get the money for the liquor complicated the situation even more.

It is also possible that the constant arguments with Yuri and the pressure she felt from taking care of two children were slowly getting to her. Yuri was not happy with their marriage since Irina would just sit around their house for hours while he worked. She didn't even try to find a job anymore but waited for his paycheck which was always unsatisfactory. Irina was probably sensing that Yuri wanted to end the marriage, so she was probably acting erratically.

The name of Irina's final victim was Alexandra Povaritsyna and she was eighty-one years old. The woman lived just down the street from the killer. The two have probably seen each other occasionally in the neighborhood and Irina was sure that the woman had some money hidden in her apartment. Irina didn't use her standard tactic of knocking on the door, introducing herself as a social worker. Instead, she offered the elderly woman her help in renovating and cleaning her apartment. The trusting woman let Irina in, expecting that she would fix her place of residence and add a breath of fresh air into her grey surroundings. However, Irina jumped on the woman almost instantly, hitting her in the head with the hammer. She didn't want to waste any time. The old lady was dead after only a couple of blows to her skull. Irina proceeded to rummage through her things in search of any hidden cash.

She didn't find much, but Irina knew that she had to leave the apartment as soon as possible. As she closed the door behind her, one of Alexandra's neighbors that lived on the same floor saw Irina and greeted her. Knowing that she was possibly identified as the killer, she exited the apartment complex walking quickly, hoping that the neighbor will not tell the police she was there. A few hours later, the murder was discovered, and the authorities were called to the scene of the crime. Recognizing the killing as the work of the serial murdered they were hunting, the investigators started talking to the tenants assuming that someone might have heard the commotion or seen someone leaving the building. They were right because the neighbor who bumped into Irina in the corridor came forward and identified the killer as one of their neighbors. The police finally had the name, and they were aware of the importance of this information. After all, they might have just solved the case that has been investigated for almost a decade.

The sensational arrest

Irina Viktorovna Gaidamachuk was arrested in June 2010, and the public in Russia was in disbelief when the identity of the killer was confirmed. She didn't resist the police and came willingly to the police station, mostly because she was aware that they had found her and had an eye-witness who could place her at the scene of her last murder. Cornered, the notorious killer who terrorized the Sverdlovsk Oblast for a total of eight years, confessed to all seventeen murders without hesitation. The police were shocked that such a small and pleasant woman was capable of these atrocious slayings of the innocent elderly women.

But one thing shocked them the most. When asked why she killed all those women, Irina simply told the detectives that her husband was not willing to give her the money for alcohol and she had to find it somewhere. She was very open about her addiction and admitted that even though the women she killed didn't have plenty of money on them, it was enough for Irina to buy vodka and get drunk when she felt the urge to do so. In the end, she stole an estimated amount of $2000 which is certainly low. It was quite unimaginable for the investigators that she was willing to hurt so many people just to get a hold of a bottle of alcoholic drink. In order to soften her confession a little bit, Irina also added that sometimes she needed the money for her children as well since her family belonged to the middle class, bordering on poverty. She was unemployed, meaning that Irina's husband provided for all four members of the family.

The police investigators didn't want to repeat the same mistake they did when they got the false confession so they talked to Irina about each and every murder she committed. She was capable of providing all the details, including the exact murder weapon used in every crime.

The investigators did find fingerprints at several crime scenes but had nothing to compare them with. Luckily, they were preserved. Once they had Irina's prints, they were the perfect match, confirming that she was actually present at several scenes. Irina was willing to talk so she also described her methods prior to the murders.

She would find lonely old women who didn't have any families, or they didn't visit them often. Once Irina found a potential target, she would spend days watching their routines and picking up small details. Everything was important, including when and where they shopped for groceries. If her victim had many visitors or friends coming over during the day, Irina would give up and find someone else. Getting caught was not an option, and she needed to know as much as possible before entering an apartment and attacking her new victim. So Irina would watch them for a very long time before actually introducing herself as a social worker.

The detectives were ready to announce that they had caught so-called Satan in a skirt. Alexander Shulga, a spokesman for Russian Investigative Committee who were at the forefront of the investigation said the following to the Russian media: *"The detainee has confessed to the murders. The proof of her guilt is that during an investigative experiment she pointed out the exact addresses where the crimes took place and described the situation including all the details. In addition, her fingerprints matched the prints left at several murder scenes."*

This discovery shocked both Irina's family and anyone who knew the woman. When interviewed for a TV news segment, one of her friends said: *"I simply cannot believe Irina is a mass murderer. She was a kind and gentle mother, always eager to help."* Irina's estranged husband Yuri filed for a divorce as soon as it was discovered that his wife was a serial killer. The two already lived apart, but Irina had the custody of the children. He was in disbelief and stated the following: *"I lived with her for 14 years but never suspected anything."* Therefore, it was clear that Irina was capable of hiding her crimes well, so it comes as no surprise that the police had such a hard time finding her. She didn't drive attention to herself and clearly didn't speak of the dark side of her personality no matter how drunk she was.

The trial and the aftermath

Suspecting that they might be dealing with an insane person, the police had to make sure Irina's mental health is fit to stand the trial. She was placed in a prison after the arrest, and the state was preparing the case against their killer. The attorneys ordered a psychological assessment that was carried out at Serbsky State Research Center for the Prevention of Traumatology. She was examined by psychiatrists and psychologists who did confirm that Irina was an addict with minor mental disturbances. But they couldn't find anything wrong with her that could suggest she was insane. The doctors concluded that the woman was aware of her actions and that she did kill each and every victim because she was sure it was the only way to get to the money. She knew that the things she was doing were wrong.

The trial began in February of 2012. The courtroom was packed with relatives and close families of all seventeen victims. They wanted justice for their loved ones. Irina was defended by Suren Sarkisyan who met her after the arrest. The prosecution had a solid case because Irina herself provided them with the details which would be more than enough to convict her. However, Irina started denying her involvement in the murders, claiming she was insane. Irina refused to take the responsibility for the killings which was unusual since she was willing to talk to the authorities the first time around. The trial that was supposed to be quite short became incredibly tiresome for everyone involved because of Irina's changing statements. It was a bit obvious to everyone that this was Sarkisyan's tactic to get his client freed of all charges.

Irina was very vocal about her innocence and did everything to make the judge see her as a disturbed individual. She was not violent but just shy. But his efforts failed because Irina was found guilty and charged with seventeen counts of murder. The prosecution managed to get a conviction for one attempted murder as well. Families and friends of the victims were satisfied at first, expecting that the judge would give Irina a life sentence, but they were unpleasantly surprised when it was announced that she would spend a total of twenty years behind the bars. Considering everything, the punishment is surprisingly short which made everyone unhappy. Claiming that the punishment for his client is too harsh, Sarkisyan announced that he will file an appeal and continue fighting for his client. Irina Viktorovna Gaidamachuk is still locked up in a prison while her legal team is doing everything they can to get her out, or at least grant her a second trial that might confirm her insanity defense.

ANATOLY THE KILLER

WALLACE SCOTT

"I'm an angel who was attending a school of Satan. Some will call me schizophrenic or even Hitler or other terrible things. That's okay with me."
- Anatoly Onoprienko

CHAPTER ONE

Anatoly Onoprienko was born in the village of Lasky in Zhtomyr Oblast in the Ukraine on July 25th, 1959. His father, Yuri Onoprienko, was a World War II hero for the Soviet Union but according to Anatoly he was abusive and an alcoholic. He also had a younger brother who was thirteen years older than him.

His mother died when he was four years old and his father sent him to live with his grandparents and aunt. The grandparents subsequently sent him to an orphanage.

Onoprienko became bitter at his family and father for sending him to the orphanage. His older brother was allowed to stay in the family home while he was sent away.

"I remember my father and brother staring at me," Onoprienko said recalling his youth. "Staring at me saying, 'let's send him to an orphanage.' I don't blame them but I'm horrified by their memory. I remember their voices."

It is unknown why Anatoly was sent to the orphanage alone while his brother remained in the care of his father. His grandmother stayed with him for the first few days there, helping him to adjust. She would eventually leave but would visit often and bring care packages of food.

A shy and quiet young boy, he did manage to make friends inside the orphanage. He would play soccer and other sports. His grades began to decline, however, as he entered the college of forestry at age fourteen.

Teachers noted a shift in his personality and became concerned. He began drinking Vodka like his father and became involved in petty thefts.

Onoprienko left the college of forestry at the age of seventeen, still unsure of what to do with his life. He joined the army in 1976 and it is here where he mastered the use of firearms. Instead of becoming a good soldier, however, he became even more alienated.

"When I was twenty years old I called myself stupid because I couldn't understand people," Onoprienko recalled. "If they were smart then I must be stupid."

Onoprienko was discharged from the army then became a sailor. He gained employment on a cruise ship in Odessa and where he would often steal money from cabins. Despite his anti-social temperament, Onoprienko had a handful of girlfriends that he would try to impress with gifts purchased with money he had stolen.

One waitress on the cruise ship caught his eye and the two began dating. She would remain his girlfriend for three years and she would give birth to his first child. Onoprienko would take a stab at being a father for awhile but discovered that it wasn't for him.

Without a word, he left his girlfriend and his baby. Onoprienko would never see them again.

"I had a unique destiny," Onoprienko said. "I had to go out and find it. I felt restless at home. Stifled. Married life wasn't for me. I needed something more."

That "something more" would be crime and murder.

CHAPTER TWO

"Onoprienko's criminal activity would increase in 1989," Ruslan Moshkovsky (Onoprienko's attorney) said. "The USSR was collapsing and no one was responsible for anything."

Onoprienko's first murder would start with his landlady.

He broke into her apartment with the goal of stealing a few pieces of jewelry. The landlady, however, came home and demanded to know what he was doing in her house.

Onoprienko panicked and shot the woman dead.

He ran out of the apartment and continued on with his life as usual. Because the police resources were so stretched out, Onoprienko was never even questioned in the murder and the crime would remain unsolved.

Onoprienko would team up with a fellow petty thief, Sergei Rogozin, and the duo would break into various residences around Kiev.

Returning home from a night of thievery, the two spotted a car pulling a trailer late one night. Onoprienko sped in front of the vehicle, blocking its route then jumped out of his car with a sawed-off shotgun in hand.

A young couple was inside and Onoprienko fired upon them without warning.

"What are you doing?" Rogozin screamed.

"Shut up!"

"I thought we were just going to rob them."

Onoprienko sprang up in Rogozin's face, caressing his cheek with the barrel of his shotgun. "If you don't shut up...If you say anything, I will kill your entire family and make you watch. Do you understand?"

Rogozin could only nod his head in agreement.

Onoprienko then buried the bodies of the couple and set fire to their car.

A month later, the two thieves gunned down another couple using the same method. Onoprienko would speed in front of the car and stop. His victims caught unaware and defenseless, Onoprienko would spring out of his car and blast away.

Rogozin would say nothing and just take whatever valuables he could find off the victims.

Onoprienko would continue accumulating his victims in this manner. He would stop families on abandoned roads and kill everyone inside. Even children.

The home burglaries continued as well with Rogozin. Onoprienko killed a family of ten people when he and Rogozin were caught in the midst of robbing their house. Two adults and eight children were killed by the duo. Onoprienko then ceased all ties with Rogozin.

"He was a kind, intelligent man," Rogozin would say later of Onoprienko. "He wasn't greedy. He seemed good-natured. I cannot say anything bad about him."

CHAPTER THREE

Onoprienko kept a low profile for a few years, moving in with a distant cousin. There are six years in his life that are unaccounted for. Some say he spent some time in a mental institution while others insist that he may be responsible for more crimes in and around the former Soviet Union. He tried to get asylum in Western Europe but failed, returning to his native Ukraine.

"He worked in Germany and Austria," Dmitry Lipsky, the trial judge said. "During our interrogation we asked if he had killed anyone there. He denied it. He said he had only committed a robbery."

"At the very beginning, I had an option to commit suicide," Onoprienko said. "And to stop this mission to kill. But then with the passage of time there was an order from above that I cannot kill myself. I'm supposed to live and keep doing what I'm doing and finish this game."

Onoprienko would return to the Ukraine in 1985 and begin a killing rampage the likes of which his country had never seen. He had anticipated that his crimes on the highway would become the stuff of legend. Instead, they were forgotten in a bureaucratic quagmire.

Not only were his crimes unknown to the general public, no one was even investigating them.

The Soviet Union had collapsed and his native state, the Ukraine, was now an independent country.

"When he came back," Moshkovsky said. "And realized that everything had been forgotten and no one was looking for him, he embarked on his second killing spree."

Like a shark circling around a minnow of fish, Onoprienko moved from town to town surveying the lay of the land. He visited some relatives who were hunters and stole a shotgun from them.

Onoprienko would saw off the barrel of the gun in order to cause maximum damage. He wanted not only to kill again but to gain notoriety for the murders.

His new crime wave started with a seventy year old woman in Odessa. He broke into her home, shot her dead then set the home on fire.

"My main purpose wasn't to rob," Onoprienko said. "My purpose was cruel. I can't explain it. My purpose was to threaten people and threaten the police. And lead them in the wrong direction."

Days later, he would travel to a town called Malyn. He skulked around the town at night and come upon a young couple having sex in their car.

"I shot at them from the driver side," Onoprienko said. "I wounded the man then the woman jumped out of the car. I waited until she put her clothes on. Then she ran off. Probably to get some help."

The woman returned shortly thereafter to check on her lover. With Onoprienko hiding near the car, he stabbed her to death. He put the woman in the car, shot the man again then drove to a secluded area where he set the car on fire.

"I started realizing that there was a plan for me," Onoprienko said. "Something was giving me direction."

CHAPTER FOUR

Onoprienko began targeting families that lived in isolated areas around Kiev. He would follow the same modus operandi in each killing. He would create a distraction, usually throwing a brick through the front window to lure the adult male(s) out of the home. Then he would kill the man of the house before entering the home and killing the wife, saving the children for last. He would then set the house on fire in order to remove all evidence. There were instances wherein witnesses would cross his path and he would kill them as well.

Onoprienko was a nocturnal killer. During the day, he played the role of the down on his luck blue collar worker but at night he would seek out fame by being a serial killer.

He would move to a town called Yavoriv, moving in with a cousin named Pyotr and his wife Yelena. Ukrainian families were communal in nature and Pyotr saw it as his duty to take care of his struggling cousin.

Pyotr's wife Yelena, however, didn't like Onoprienko. She knew that there was something 'off' about the man and felt uneasy when she discovered the rifle under his bed.

Yelena pressured her husband into kicking Onoprienko out of the house. Pyotr could not throw his cousin out on the streets but he decided instead to play matchmaker. He knew a hair dresser that was recently divorced and looking for a decent man to be her meal ticket. Pyotor threw a family party, invite the woman over and she immediately hit it off with Onoprienko.

The woman was named Ana Kazak. She had two children of her own but her ex-husband was an alcoholic. She an attraction to the soft-spoken Onoprienko and the two began living together.

Onoprienko told his new live-in girlfriend that he was a "traveling businessman" and she never questioned his long absences from home.

Onoprienko would travel all the way to Malyn which was a town that was often hit by blackouts. He would be able to get in and out, do his killings under the cloak of night when no one had electricity nor did they have the capability to call for help. It was the perfect scenario for the serial killer.

CHAPTER FIVE

It was Christmas Eve when Onoprienko came upon the secluded home of the Zaichenko family which was located in the small village of Garmarnia. Inside, a forestry teacher lived along with his wife and two sons.

Onoprienko crept around the exterior of the home, found a ladder and propped it against the wall. He climbed up to the bedroom window and fired through the glass, killing the father and three year old son who was sleeping with him.

"I just shot them," Onoprienko said. "It's not that it gave me pleasure, but I felt this urge. From then on, it was almost like some game from outer space."

Onoprienko then jumped through the window and went from room to room.

"Don't kill us!" the wife pleaded as Onoprienko came through her door. He stabbed the woman and then strangled their three-month old baby.

"I didn't want to waste bullets on the weak," Onoprienko said.

He then ripped the wedding rings off the couple's hands as well as taking a small golden cross on a chain, earrings and clothes before torching the home.

Onoprienko would later say that he had "a vision from God" and was ordered to murder.

"When we arrived at the site, we were in shock," Leonid Martynenko, lead investigator of the Zaichenko murder said. "We discovered that the whole family had died violently. At the time, we didn't know the reason for the crime. We developed leads, examined a number of options. We considered burglary the main motive then. We thought it was homicide for purpose of robbery."

Onoprienko returned home and spent Christmas with Ana and her two sons. On New Year's Eve, however, the told her that he had to "go away on business."

Onoprienko would then travel to the town of Bratkovichi where he would indulge in his killing fantasies once again.

The streets of the town were deserted at night and Onoprienko was getting antsy. Then in the distance, he saw a man walking down the street.

"How you doing?" Onoprienko asked the man. "Was wondering if you could spare me a dollar or two so I can get something to eat?"

"Get the fuck away from me, you bum!" the man said. He was dressed in a forestry uniform and looked to be going home from work.

"Just a dollar."

"Fuck you!"

The man turned around and Onoprienko shot him in the back. The forester fell face first to the ground. Onoprienko quickly dragged the man to the side of the road. He rifled through his pockets, taking his money and keys. Then he stripped the man naked.

The night was just getting started for Onoprienko as he continued his rampage throughout the town. He noticed a man hanging curtains in his window and Onoprienko fired away, killing the man. Breaking into the home, he killed the man's wife and her twin sisters that were also living there. He then cut off the wife's finger and stole her wedding ring.

"It was like cutting through a tree branch," Onoprienko said. "It was very easy. Cutting through flesh was like cutting through butter."

He could not help but stop to admire his handiwork before he set the house ablaze.

"I was observing the victims," Onoprienko said. "Those who were already killed. How they were killed or were dying. Or how they were living the last minutes of their lives."

Onoprienko hopped on the train and returned home. When he got home, he took the wedding ring off the dead woman's finger and proposed to Ana.

"After the second murder we knew we had a maniac on our hands," Martynenko said. "We came to the location and viewed the scene. We saw the brutality of the crime and it had become absolutely clear to us that it was the same man that committed all the killings."

Gathering and sharing information still proved to be a problem in the Ukraine. Old Soviet style narratives were still being adhered to, like that of the government never admitting that serial killers existed in their country. It was part of the old Soviet style propaganda, wanting to prove to the world that killings didn't take place in their Communist territory. Even though the Ukraine was now free from such commandments, the leadership still adhered to keeping information away from the public and not admitting that they had a problem.

"It was striking how systematic the murders were," Romanyuk said. "There were group murders. Whole families were wiped out for no visible reason. That was really astounding."

Four days later after his marriage proposal, Onoprienko began gunning people down on the Berdyansk, Dnieprovskaya highway. He stopped cars, feigning as if he needed assistance then he would shoot the drivers. The victims were Kasai, a Navy ensign, a taxi driver named Savitsky, a kolkhoz cook named Kochergina and another unidentified victim.

"To me it was like hunting," Onoprienko said. "Hunting people down. I would be sitting, bored, with nothing to do. And then suddenly this idea would get into my head. I would do everything to get it out of my mind, but I couldn't. It was stronger than me. So I would get in the car or catch a train and go out to kill."

Onoprienko waited another eleven days, take a train to the village of Bratkovichi and invading the home of the Pilat family. He would shoot all five family members in the home and once again set fire to the place. He would be seen by two witnesses and he promptly killed them both.

"I look at it very simply," Onoprienko said. ""As an animal, I watched all this as an animal would stare at sheep."

The blood lust now running freely, Onoprienko could not refrain himself from killing.

On January 30th, 1996, Onoprienko killed a nurse named Marusina, her two sons and a family friend in Fastova, Kieskaya Oblast region of the Ukraine.

"I could not stop myself," he would say later to investigators. "I became obsessed with killing. To me killing people is like ripping up a duvet. Men, women, old people, children, they are all the same. I have never felt sorry for those I killed. No love, no hatred, just blind indifference. I don't see them as individuals, but just as masses."

Onoprienko would continue to take small items from the homes as souvenirs before going back home. He would bring his fiancee clothes, jewelry and a tape deck which he presented as gifts.

On February 19th , 1996, Onoprienko invaded the home of the Dubchak family. He shot and killed the father and son then bludgeoned the mother to death with a hammer. The family had a daughter, and he walked into her room to find her praying.

"Where do your parents keep the money!" he demanded.

The girl looked at her killer straight in the eye, defiant.

"Show me where the money is!"

"No, I won't," the girl said.

Onoprienko then killed the girl.

'That strength (the girl's) was incredible," Onoprieko said. "But I felt nothing."

Onoprienko then broke into the home of the Bodnarchuck family in Malina, Lvivskaya Oblast. He started with his usual tactic of throwing a rock at the door. The father, however, came out of the home with an ax. Onoprienko promptly shot the man and then the wife who came to the door to investigate the noise. Onoprienko then went inside and chopped up the daughters with the ax. A neighbor named Tsalk wandered onto the property and Onoprienko shot him to death before chopping up his body as well.

"Oh, you know, I killed them because I loved them so much," Onoprienko said. "Those children, those men and women, I had to kill them, the inner voice spoke inside my mind and heart and pushed me so hard!"

On March 22nd, 1996, Onoprienko shot and killed members of the Novosad family. He then set the house on fire to remove all traces of evidence.

"He would always set the places on fire," Romanyuk said. "People saw the fire and came to fight it. There was no evidence left only holes in the walls and cartridges."

Police would use forensic science to discover that the holes in the walls were left by a hunting weapon, specifically a gun that had the barrel sawed off.

"I'm not a maniac," Onoprienko said. "If I were, I would have thrown myself onto you and killed you right here. No, it's not that simple. I have been taken over by a higher force, something telepathic or cosmic, which drove me. I am like a rabbit in a laboratory. A part of an experiment to prove that man is capable of murdering and learning to live with his crimes. To show that I can cope, that I can stand anything, forget everything."

The Ukrainian government could no longer keep a lid on the killings. Rumors had spread of a man who was on a rampage throughout the entire country, murdering families at random.

The people of the region all lived in fear. Some families would stay together at night and press their furniture up against the door at night.

"People would come home from work early," said one Ukrainian resident. "People were scared to death. Students who were away at college quickly came home to be with their parents. I had one neighbor that put bars on their windows. Everyone was scared."

The press had given him the nickname of "The Terminator."

Onoprienko had achieved his goal. He had become the most feared man in his country.

CHAPTER SIX

The Ukrainian military patrolled certain villages to keep the people safe. Schools near the murders were shut down as a precaution. There was daily radio updates and a lot of the citizens likened the experience to being in a war.

"All the police departments were given specific instructions as to what to look for," Romanyuk said. "They knew how the killer behaved, that he acted at night. They investigated any sound. Even when a dog barked at night. The orders were strict."

The Ukraine launched a sweeping manhunt, determined to find the killer. They were convinced that this was the work of one man and dispensed their National Guard plus over 2,000 police investigators on the case.

"We had special teams of different officers working in different capacities," Bodgan Romanyuk, the chief of police said. "We had officers in the field, around-the-clock gathering information and working with operatives. Then there were others who in charge of strategy, who conducted the ground operations."

Later that month, the Security Service of Ukraine (SBU) and the Public Prosecutor's Office specialists arrested a 26-year old man named Yury Mozola, thinking he was responsible for the family murders. Over the course of three days, seven Ukrainian law enforcement officials tortured the young man, employing burning, electrocution and beatings.

Mozola, however, refused to confess and would later die during the torture.

The seven men were then prosecuted for the murder and sentenced to jail.

Days later after Mozola's death, Onoprienko was finally captured after a massive manhunt.

An anonymous caller gave police a tip on Onoprienko. He said that he witnessed him trying to conceal a shotgun as he left his apartment building.

Police then surrounded Onoprienko's building, staking out every possible exit until storming the apartment.

"It was quite risky," Romanyuk said. "Because on the one hand there was no evidence. But, on the other hand, what if it's him? What if it is this trained killer who shoots people dead on the spot and our officers are only human."

"We had learned that our suspect was anti-social. He wouldn't open the door to anyone. It was Easter and his fiance went to visit her mother, out of town. She would return in the evening and when we rang we'd hope that he'd think that it was her coming home."

The police came to the door and knocked.

Opening the door was a small man with red hair.

He opened the door calmly, expecting his girlfriend.

The police forced their way in and demanded his identification.

Onoprienko then reached for his gun but the police overpowered him, grabbing his wrists. Wresting the pistol away, they identified it as one that had been stolen from a crime scene.

Searching the man for his identification, they recognized him as Anatoly Onoprienko.

"In the apartment is everything," Romanyuk said. "All the evidence is there. Things from the crime scenes where he murdered people in different regions."

The police officers held up the numerous guns and knives to his face.

"It isn't mine!" the killer protested. "All that stuff doesn't belong to me."

His fiancee Ana, return home. She was shocked to see Onoprienko being arrested as she maintained that he had been the sweetest man she had ever met and had been nothing but nice to her and her two children.

The police, however, disputed her notions by showing her the weapons that he had stashed in her apartment.

"I started talking with his fiancee," Romanyuk recalled. "And I tried to find ways of connecting him with these murders. We were able to match dates. She would give us a date when he wasn't home for a day or two and that date would correspond with the murders."

The police searched through the apartment and found over one-hundred twenty-two items that were taken from the crime scenes. Guns and knives all matched what they were looking for in terms of murder weapons.

After the debacle with the previous suspect, the police authorities wanted proof beyond a shadow of a doubt.

"For me," Romanyuk said. "It was crucial that it we were sure that it was him. To make sure that he could be tied to these killings."

The police brought the killer into the station and interrogated him until six o'clock in the morning. Onoprienko denied all involvement until he finally cracked early in the morning.

"I was commanded by God to kill," Onoprienko told his interrogators. "I was chosen because I'm a superior specimen. I have the power of hypnosis and can call animals through telepathy. I can stop and start my heart with my mind."

He told of being diagnosed with schizophrenia and being admitted to a hospital in Kiev.

"He told us about all fifty-two murders he committed," Romanyuk said. "Not only the ones he performed in 1995 but also about the murders he committed in the past a long time ago."

Onoprienko expressed relief at being caught. He had grew tired of killing and being covered in blood all the time.

The police then turned Onoprienko over to the Ukrainian interior ministry.

Upon his transference to this higher authority, Onoprienko immediately began making demands.

"Give me a box of candy," Onoprienko said. "Sausages and some crackers. Otherwise I won't talk to you."

Onoprienko was then allowed to take advantage of a strange quirk in Ukrainian law. In the Ukraine, a trial cannot commence until the defendant has read all of the evidence against him.

At his leisure.

Onoprienko was obligated to read over volumes of police reports and crime scene photos. There were over fifty-two dead bodies, some dismembered and burned. Finally, he relented and after seven months he led the police to the areas where he had killed his victims. Onoprienko would detail each murder with an eery calmness, remarking at how easy it was for him to kill his victims.

There was another delay in that the Ukraine would have to transport, feed and house all of the witnesses who came from different parts of the country. Ultimately, there would be no witnesses testifying at his trial as some of the family members did not want to come forth.

A full three years after his apprehension, Onoprienko was finally brought to trial. Onoprienko was forced to sit in court in an iron cage. People spat upon him and threatened to tear him apart.

"I'm a person, a regular person," Onoprienko said. "Anybody can become a murderer. I was helped. It either it a God or the devil. Whatever he calls himself."

"He needs to be shot!" screamed a woman in the court room.

"He does not deserve to be shot!" screamed another. "He needs to die a slow and agonizing death."

The trial drew national publicity and the security around the courtroom was tight.

Judge Dmytro Lypsky asked Onoprienko if he had anything to say.

"No, nothing," the killer said shrugging his shoulders.

"You have been informed of our legal rights-"

"It's your law," he growled.

"State your nationality," the judge said.

"None."

"That's impossible."

"According to the police," Onoprienko said. "I'm Ukrainian."

"Do you have anything else to say in your defense?"

"I've been a robot for years," the killer said. "Driven by dark forces. I should not be put on trial until authorities can determine the force. You are not able to take me as I am. You do not see all the good I'm going to do! And you will never understand me. This is a great force that controls this hall as well. You will never understand this. Maybe only your grandchildren will understand.

Onoprienko was cooperative throughout the trial until the end. He requested that his state-appointed lawyer, Ruslan Mashkovsky, be replaced by someone who was "at least 50 years old, Jewish or half-Jewish, economically independent and has international experience."

The court refused his request. He was confined to a metal cage inside the courtroom as the rest of the proceedings took place.

"I started preparing for prison life a long time ago," Onoprienko recalled. "I fasted, did yoga, I am not afraid of death," Onoprienko said. "Death for me is nothing. Naturally, I would prefer the death penalty. I have absolutely no interest in relations with people. I have betrayed them. The first time I killed, I shot down a deer in the woods. I was in my early twenties and I recall feeling very upset when I saw it dead. I couldn't explain why I had done it and I felt sorry for it. I never had that feeling again."

The closing arguments began in April of 1999. Prosecutor Yury Ignatenko pressed for the death sentence while Moshkovsky would try to bring up Onoprienko's childhood to generate his sympathy.

"My defendant was deprived of motherly love since the age of four," Moshkovsky argued. "And the absence of care which is necessary for the formation of a real man. I appeal to the court to soften the punishment."

Moshkovsky himself, however, knew that Onoprienko was the epitome of evil, saying and doing things for dramatic effect.

"He was a cunning, shrewd and a great psychologist," Moshkovsky said later. "He was hard to catch because he acted alone and without accomplices. He was a butcher, killing defenseless and poor people. He specifically chose villages on the outskirts where there was no telephone, where even cars pass with difficulty. Even if someone heard a shot, there would be no one to call."

After only three hours of deliberation, the judge sentenced Onoprienko to death by shooting.

"I've robbed and killed," Onoprienko said in his final statement. "But I'm a robot, I don't feel anything. I've been close to death so many times that it's even interesting for me now to venture into the after world, to see what is there, after this death."

The Ukraine, however, had just joined the Council of Europe and had committed to abolishing capital punishment.

Onoprienko was then spared the death penalty even though he gave the President of the Ukraine a personalized letter that he would kill again.

"If I am ever let out, I will start killing again," Onoprienko wrote. "But this time it will be worse, ten times worse. The urge is there. Seize this chance because I am being groomed to serve Satan. After what I have learnt out there, I have no competitors in my field. And if I am not killed I will escape from this jail and the first thing I'll do is find Kuchma (the Ukrainian president) and hang him from a tree by his testicles."

The Terminator would die of heart failure in the prison of Zhytomyr on August 27th, 2013 at the age of 54.

MANIAC

FRANK COLEMAN

*Stranger than **Fiction***

In 2010, journalist Denis Faye sat down with industry expert Pat Brown in an attempt to bridge the gap between how serial killers are portrayed in film and television and how they are in real life. Brown quickly cuts through the existing information floating around on this disparity.

> *"Faye: So what does Hollywood get right about serial killers?*
> *Brown: Very little."*

In the case of "real life" serial killer Alexander Pichushkin, known as the infamous Bitsa Maniac, the Chessboard Killer, and arguably one of Russia's most consummate serial killer, it's almost impossible to draw the line between fact and fiction. Between his mysterious past, the inventiveness of the press, and his own fabrications, Pichushkin's story requires an eye for the difference between killers from the silver screen and true monsters.

Described as a "real-life criminal profiler," Pat Brown has a lot to say about the difference between the fictional serial killers we see in movies and television and the all too real murderers we catch glimpses of in the news. In an interview with the WGA, she attempted to outline some of the most prominent errors writers make when depicting serial killers. She immediately honed in on the false complexity that writers default to in order to create drama, lamenting that such specificity is almost never the case.

> *"They're not as bizarre as the films show... [They] tend to over-profile the killer's mental state."*

In the news, Alexander Pichushkin's story has been sensationalized and stretched, the gaps in his narrative filled with fiction. Between 1992 and 2006 Pichushkin was responsible for the deaths of up to

62 people, putting him in the running for being one of Russia's most prolific serial killers. But despite this infamy and attention, there are plenty of holes in the account of his killing spree for reporters to expound and invent. Even Pichushkin's Wikipedia entry contains an entirely fictional tale of his childhood inspired solely by his title as the Chessboard Killer. This moniker may be the most popular and certainly most evocative option for Pichushkin, but it is by no means the most accurate. Those who were most affected by this slew of murders and know the most about them, locals and experts alike, all prefer the more succinct and accurate name Pichushkin had earned: the Maniac.

Creating a **Monster**

Psychologists often argue whether the monstrousness of serial killers is born or made by trauma or environment. On one hand, being able to point a finger at exactly what caused a human being to do such horrible things can be comforting, but all too often external factors are used to distance killers from blame and evoke sympathy. Brown laments that this distancing is what she is most opposed to in the portrayal of serial killers. "I've never seen a serial killer with redeeming qualities or one you can have some kind of sympathy for, like it's just a bad hobby he's got." On the other hand, a world with the potential for people who are simply born to commit heinous murders is a scary one to imagine, and given the number of environmental similarities between serial killers, one that frankly doesn't seem to exist.

Currently, the prevailing argument is that it is a combination of the natural and nurtured elements of someone's personality that react upon one another to create a psychopath, though Brown feels there is more of a conscious choice involved. "He's just pissed off at society and became a psychopath when life didn't work out his way..." In the case of Pichushkin, close analysis of his childhood, family, and early social interactions reveal many of the trademarks common in other serial killers, however, Brown's reminder of free will is an important one to keep in mind. While Pichushkin's childhood has some traumatic roots, ultimately he was not *made* into a monster—he *chose* to commit murder, and on a minimum of 52 separate occasions.

On April 9th, 1974 Alexander Pichushkin was born in Mytishchi, Moscow, and according to his mother, Natasha Pichushkina, he was a normal child as far as she could tell. Alexander, or Sasha for short, lived in a modest one bedroom apartment with his father and mother who had grown up in that same apartment. The complex is one of many on the outskirts of Moscow, a decaying remainder of soviet era infrastructure and some of the only reasonably priced housing in the area. Nicknamed *khrushchevki* after Nikita Khrushchev, the spartan public housing lacks charm and personality, but continues to serve in functionality and affordability. A mere nine months after Sasha is born, his father leaves Natasha to raise their son alone.

"I tried to raise him like a normal mother... I know now that I raised my son very poorly... [but] I can't say what I did wrong."

Besides his mother's account in a popular interview from 2007, not much is known about young Sasha's childhood. One of the few verified details of Sasha's childhood is the head trauma he incurred at the age of four when he fell backward off a swing outside the *khrushchevki* only for it to swing toward him again and strike his forehead. Immediately following the incident he spent time in an institution for the disabled, though exactly how long he stayed there is not reported. Brain injuries, specifically to the frontal lobe where Sasha was struck, are very common among serial killers. David Berkowitz, Leonard Lake, Kenneth Bianchi, and John Gacy all suffered similar head trauma early in life, which neuroscientists link to violence and impulse control issues, as well as emotional and empathetic difficulties.

There are plenty of other mixed and unsubstantiated accounts of torment in Sasha's childhood inflicted by bullies instead of by accident, including one anecdote about a group of children ganging up on Sasha to steal his moped. A police investigator offered a possible explanation in an interview, saying that "Pichushkin" is a name with an effeminate, weak connotation, a detail that would otherwise be lost to the cultural barrier. Entrenched in a Russian cultural context often tinged with homophobia and toxic ideas of masculinity, young Sasha had his cards stacked against him. With the effeminate name, an absent father, a stint in an institution, and very few, if any, friends, he was ideal fodder for grade school bullies. Despite Pichushkin eventually outgrowing his childhood weaknesses and becoming a model image of Russian masculinity, many experts speculate that he might not be heterosexual.

Mentioned only briefly in an interview with the lead investigator, the question of the Bitsa Maniac's sexuality was quickly brushed off. Pichushkin smoked and drank, had a menial physical job stocking shelves at a grocery store, and a low voice with a gruff personality—to those surrounded by the cultural context of Russia's now-infamous homophobia, there was no possible way he could be anything but straight. Add in the brutal success of his murderous impulses and there is no hope of swaying the investigation's narrow image of Pichushkin.

His mother Natasha brought up in her 2007 interview that he never seemed to be interested in women or sex in general. His only documented emotional attachment is to a male classmate from his teens. An overwhelming majority of his victims, the people he was able to lure most easily and was most comfortable with, are all male ranging from as young as nine years old to retirement age. While there was never evidence of any sexual assault on his male victims to substantiate any of these claims, there also was a complete lack of sexual activity with his female victims as well. Based on the available, though sparse, information, it seems just as likely that Sasha lacked sexual impulse at all, and instead only had a lust to kill.

Yet another facet in the claims against Pichushkin's heterosexuality, young Sasha seemed to be heavily influenced by another serial killer, Andrei Chikatilo, whom he idolized to the extreme. Chikatilo's crimes came to light just as Sasha reached his most consciously formative years, and he kept careful track of his contemporary's every move. Chikatilo's spree of murders earned him the nickname of the Rostov Ripper, but he, like Sasha, was deemed by the press a maniac.

Finding *Inspiration*

In December of 1991 the newly liberated Russian media received news of an arrest made in relation to the series of unsolved, gruesome murders happening 117 miles northeast of Moscow, in Rostov von don. For nearly a decade the area had been terrorized by murders that were clearly linked to the same killer, who had been referred to as the Rostov Ripper. Immediately after the arrest, sensationalist news sources had yet to learn his name or see his photo, but had a brief summary of his crimes. His signature was stabbing, usually in excess of 30 times, gouging of the eyes, sexual assault, and evisceration; accused of 53 counts of murder in this style, the man whose name would later be learned became simply *the Maniac*. The public did not lay eyes upon the monster that they knew so little about until he appeared at the first day of his trial on April 14th the following year.

Just five days after Sasha's eighteenth birthday the media is suddenly saturated with the face of the Rostov Ripper, now revealed to be Andrei Chikatilo. His sallow face is pictured from behind iron bars throughout the trial, specially put in place of the usual plexiglass box, to protect him from the often hysterical and retaliatory relatives of his victims. These attacks were not the only noteworthy outbursts of the trial: Chikatilo and the judge, Leonid Akubzhanov, remained combative toward each other throughout the proceedings, with Chikatilo refusing to cooperate. Ignoring questions posed by the prosecution, Chikatilo's original well-spoken demeanor devolved into a show-stopping display of chaos, singing socialist anthems and exposing himself to the jury in an attempt to be deemed unfit to stand trial.

As the trial continued into the summer, news outlets revealed more of Chikatilo's gory past, full of sexual assault while in his teaching position, torturous excess during his killings, and the numerous occasions he was apprehended, questioned, or suspected before his final arrest. Sasha followed all of these stories with more than the morbid curiosity typical of a boy his age. He clipped articles from the papers and kept photos of Chikatilo's face, images with captions that described him as a "shaven-skulled demon" and articles detailing the horrific, decade long murder spree of *the Maniac.*

With the clarity of hindsight, Pichushkin's serial murders appear to be somewhat spawned from Chikatilo's, if not directly inspired. Teenaged Sasha was exposed to widespread press coverage of his killings and saw the attention he garnered from the public and his victims' families. He witnessed the controversy over Chikatilo's punishment, which arguably contributed to the suspension of Russia's death penalty in 1996 (notably, after executing yet another serial killer, Sergey Golovkin). At the very least, Pichushkin seemed intent on surpassing Chikatilo in number, keeping track of his alleged 61 victims with numbers pasted on his now-infamous chessboard. While journalists after the fact like to fixate on this chessboard and invent a final goal of filling it with 64 murders, Pichushkin never mentioned the board in his taped confession. Motivated only by his need to kill and desire to overshadow the Rostov Ripper, the lead police investigator doubted Pichushkin would stop when he ran out of squares.

"Pichushkin is quite an unusual serial killer he's a hunter, a typical hunter and his only motivation was to kill, there was no other motive, whatever else we might have thought."

*A New **Maniac** Begins*

On the 27th of July, Sasha takes his first step towards becoming the infamous Bitsa Maniac. Now three months after turning eighteen years old, he invites his friend and classmate Mikhail Odichuck to join him in something he has been ruminating possibly for years: to commit his first murder. For Pichushkin, this is the most intimate gesture he could possibly offer. Only a trusted friend, a confidante, someone he would deem worthy of sharing such a powerful experience of control and subversion of societal expectations could have been welcomed so wholly into Sasha's inner circle. Unfortunately for both boys, what Sasha viewed as a generous offer, Mikhail saw as a joke.

It would be easy to jump to the conclusion that Sasha held some form of fondness or affection towards his classmate Mikhail. With the seeming absence of his sexual attraction to women in combination with idolization of Chikatilo and experience being bullied as a child, their relationship could have even been interpreted as a boyhood crush. Out of 51 charges of murder and attempted murder, only three victims were female, a statistic that belies Pichushkin's gravitation toward men in general. At such an important developmental stage in his life, Sasha would be expected to display sexual and emotional attraction towards those he felt closest to at the time, namely his friend Mikhail. With over a decade of experience in examining the personalities of serial killers, specialist Pat Brown would insist otherwise.

"What people don't get is that a psychopath can portray, at certain points in his life, certain levels of affection... [but] those are just objects in his life... People are either useful, or they're in the way."

Mikhail made the mistake of getting in the way. Eventually the boy realized Sasha was dedicated to the idea of murder—and completely prepared. He knew to prey on the elderly and the homeless, strangers, who wouldn't be missed by family or valued by the police enough to warrant further investigation. He had already crafted the story of his "beloved" dog's grave in Bitsa Park as a trick to lure their victims with promise of a free drink, both lowering their victim's guard and impeding their ability to fight back. Most importantly, Sasha had discovered the manholes in Bitsa Park that fell up to 18 meters deep, full of highly pressurized currents, in which he would later dispose of twenty to thirty bodies. At exactly what point Mikhail came to the realization that Sasha was deadly serious, only Pichushkin knows—but his classmate never made it to the forest. That Monday afternoon Mikhail's lifeless body is found in the street, after dropping from a five-story balcony. Young Sasha was questioned by police, but they never suspected his involvement and ruled the tragedy a suicide with little to no other inquiry.

Prompted by Pichushkin's confession fifteen years later, a follow-up investigation examined Mikhail's body and discovered head trauma that didn't fit within expectations of impact on the ground. What they had glossed over appeared to be evidence that 18 year old Sasha had bashed in his classmate's head up to 21 times with an unidentifiable blunt object before lifting his lifeless body over the edge of the balcony to drop into the street below. Though the final result is similar to the neat, premeditated M.O. he would adopt later in life, this first murder was a crime of passion, fueled by betrayal and rage, and a moment Pichushkin would later look back on fondly.

"This first murder," he began in his televised confession, "It's like first love—It's unforgettable."

An Experimental Phase

For the next nine years, Pichushkin waits. Investigators speculated that Sasha repressed his homicidal urges for as long as possible, knowing that he would not be able to stop once he started again. Pichushkin neither confirmed nor denied these claims, and has offered no other explanation for such a long hiatus. But after those nine years are up, Sasha embarks on a personal journey with an astonishing body count, to discover all the ways he can kill and all the ways he can get away with it.

Now at the age of 27, Sasha began to mix up his M.O., experimenting with weapons, victims, and body disposal. The homeless were his first choice of victims, on whom he tested out another toss over the balcony and a homemade "pen shooter" Sasha had crafted himself; Pichushkin lamented in an interview that both of these methods were over too quickly. This second falling victim was only nine years old, whose death was overlooked just like Mikhail's. As for the pen shooter incident, Pichushkin later described the murder in his confession with explicit detail, from finding a homeless man sleeping on the street, to pressing the makeshift gun to his temple in broad daylight and watching him bleed. He explained that he had seen the man as an opportunity while he was walking to work and couldn't resist.

Eventually he moved on to victims who needed to be lured into the cover of the park, but these still would not be the bodies found by police and attributed to the Bitsa Maniac. The story Sasha told many of his victims centered on a "beloved" deceased dog, whose grave, he told them, was in the park. He would offer a drink of vodka over the nonexistent burial site to distract and relax them; little did they know that the spot he lead them to was strategically located by one of the manholes he had discovered in his youth. Sasha would then bash their heads on the manhole cover, only to open it and lift their inebriated or even unconscious bodies over the edge. His story varied slightly each time, and he continued to use opportunities like the sleeping homeless man to take advantage of poor drunks who wouldn't be missed amid his more focused strategy. Yet another distinction between fact and fiction, where news outlets attempted to fit all of Pichushkin's murders into a neat little box, Brown argues that just isn't so.

"[A real serial killer] doesn't have a fantastic signature with every crime, something really creepy that links every one of the crimes together … It's very exciting, but it's not the way it is in real life. He's not always going to use the same method. He might try something else on another day, so you have to be careful of that."

When he later told police of his use of the sewer system to dispose of the corpses, they tested its validity by dropping a mannequin inside, only for it to be immediately torn apart by the forceful currents. They also later found the body of a missing person whose death Pichushkin had claimed fault of further into the system. Pichushkin blamed the police force's ineptitude for not being able to find the bodies he had so effectively destroyed. Normally the police would have to rely on what little evidence they have to corroborate a murderer's often fantastical claims and any particulars are reliant on the trustworthiness of a murderer. In Pichushkin's case, his haste to kill left three survivors in his wake who told police and the press every minute detail.

The first to live to tell the tale was Maria Viricheva, who was pregnant at the time of her attempted murder. Pichushkin met her in a metro station on February 23rd 2002 and must have been able to recognize that she was in pressing financial need. He crafted a story of cameras he had hidden away in a manhole in Bitsa Park, offering to sell them to her at a discount so she might turn a profit. Desperate, Maria accepted and followed him into the forest. At the opening to the sewer, Maria quickly realized her mistake as Pichushkin grabbed her and beat her head against the lid, which he then opened and dropped her inside. Miraculously, Maria maintained consciousness, and gripped the slippery walls while attempting to regain some strength amidst the freezing currents. Maria estimated that she spent almost 20 hours trapped in the sewer, struggling between trying to find a way to climb out and her fading will to live. Eventually she discovered rungs that lead to another manhole and was able to climb out to safety.

In addition to Maria, 13 year old Mikhail Lobov fell victim to Pichushkin's invitation to the park for a free drink and cigarettes. Mikhail was just one of many in a crowd of leather jackets and piercings, often hanging around the metro stations, loitering in front of food stands, and drinking. Investigators were unable to find any footage of Mikhail and Pichushkin together in the metro station nearest Bitsa Park, but they still speculate that the most likely place they met would be there. Once in the park, Mikhail's story reads like just like the others—an offer of vodka over the imaginary dog's grave, head meets manhole cover, and into the sewer he goes. The exception to the normal script comes when Mikhail's leather jacket catches on a piece of metal rather high up in the sewer, and his fall is stopped before he even reaches the water. Completely unaware, Pichushkin leaves the park thinking he killed the boy. Just moments later, Mikhail is able to crawl out shaken and disturbed, but with only minor head injuries.

Possibly the most unsettling part of these survivors' stories is when they turn to the local police to report their attacker, only to be turned away. Hospitalized and having just received news that she lost her pregnancy, Maria Viricheva frantically described the entire ordeal from beginning to end, including a full description of Pichushkin's appearance. Instead of taking action, police ignored her account and instead asked for her citizenship documentation. Maria didn't have any, and the police generously offerto ignore the whole situation, leaving her injured and alone in a hospital with Pichushkin continuing his murder spree.

When Mikhail went to police, they brushed him off as a lying punk and told him to go home. Not a month later, Mikhail ran into Pichushkin in a crowded metro station and began yelling and pulling at his hair in frustration, dragging his attacker over to a policeman standing guard and demanding vindication. The officer escorted

Mikhail out of the station and told him again just to go home. Possibly even worse is the third survivor case, of a middle aged homeless man whose story has continued to be ignored and undocumented, even in the wake of Pichushkin's conviction.

Corroborated by these detailed survivor accounts, Pichushkin's confession weaves in the rest of the story. While the sewer was serving him well for body disposal, he still wasn't getting the satisfaction he was looking for. Instead of simply using the manhole cover, Sasha escalated to bringing a yellow-handled utility hammer with him to bash in the skulls of his victims before throwing them in the sewer. At this point, around thirty people had gone missing from his neighborhood. Police still weren't interested in the goings-on of the lower class, but the local gossip had begun to gain footing and Sasha wanted credit for his work.

The Hunt for the **Bitsa Maniac**

It's not until August 15th, 2005 that the police discover their first body, deep in Bittsevsky Park. The victim was a 31 year old man named Nikolai Wirogiev, who had suffered extensive head trauma and, most shockingly, had a vodka bottle lodged in the wound. Law enforcement officer Denis Adamenko was one of the first on the scene; years later he is still able to pinpoint the exact place the first body was found, and describe the scene with gruesome detail. Though he had no idea what was in store at the time of the first police-documented murder, Adamenko would continue working on the case from the first body to Pichushkin's trial.

One month later, another man with the same injuries is found in the park. Just two weeks after that yet another body is found, and then again after only one week. Very suddenly the police began to link the murders together, realizing these stranger killings had to be the handiwork of a single killer. Though the vodka bottle signature isn't present every time, bodies begin piling up within the same age range and sex, all with substantial brain injuries. Sometimes in lieu of a vodka bottle, sticks are found in the wounds, but the reasoning for their presence remains the same: Sasha now likes to play with his victims after the fact.

Brown's interview offers some further insight into Pichushkin's newest escalation, explaining that the often-overlooked element of power is usually what creates specific signatures, such as the vodka bottle or sticks, instead of overly complex motives. "It's just that the fun ends too quickly, so instead of walking away from the body, they want to play with it because they can continue having control. *Now I'm eating you! Look at that!* It's an ongoing feeling of power."

In November of 2005 the police receive a wake up call in the form of the brutalized body and fifth victim of the unknown serial killer, a man named Nikolai Zakharchenko who was a 63 year old pensioner and an ex-cop. Like many of Pichushkin's victims, Zakharchenko lived in the same *khrushchevki* with his family, just two doors down from his murderer. Up until this point, every victim had been part of the underprivileged lower class, either homeless without family or deemed low priority by biased police. Claiming Pichushkin consciously targeted members of society that would not be missed or investigated, as some news sources allege, would be giving him far too much credit. An opportunist at heart, Sasha simply killed whenever he had the chance, with no regard for background or lack thereof, leading to the critical mistake of killing the former policeman. It's only at this point that police give the case with an accumulating body count over to an elite murder squad within the force. What the investigators don't know is that the fifth body that they've found is actually the 41st murder Sasha would later be convicted of.

By the beginning of the next year, news of a serial killer in Moscow had been upgraded from rumors among the working class to front page news. Reports from the Moscow Times warned residents of murders in

Bittsevsky Park, introducing the nickname 'Bitsa Maniac' for the first time. Pichushkin's half sister Katya, who lived in the same apartment as Sasha with her husband and child, later discussed in an interview seeing a news reel about the Maniac on tv and panicking for her brother's safety. It was well known that Sasha frequented the park, but she recalls he was never afraid that there was a killer on the loose. Meanwhile, the body count continued to rise.

*A **Red Herring** in Bitsa Park*

In a fit of desperation, both the police and the general public began speculating wildly about the killer's possible identity. The investigation's gaze soon turned to the sanitarium looming suggestively on the edge of Bitsa Park. Many of the patients at the ward had privileges that included the freedom to leave the building during the day without aid, and police could not help but notice that the dumping grounds fell well within walking distance. Officers immediately restricted this freedom pending further inquiry; what began as a series of interviews eventually escalated into the interrogation of every single patient with the means to walk to the park. Eventually this branch of the investigation ceased, producing no leads or valid suspects.

By mid-February, a series of sensational rumors arose fueled purely by the area's vicious homophobia. Whispers citing evidence that never existed and eyewitness accounts simply looking for their five minutes of fame circulated not from the humble residents of the *khrushchevki,* but from the panicked upper middle class. Suddenly past visitors to the park came out of the woodwork, claiming they saw the killer fleeing through the trees and describing him as a man in women's clothing and a wig. Yet another piece of gossip spread claiming some of the bodies had been raped and found with lipstick marks all over the face, neck, and body.

Demonstrating they are not immune to the rampant homophobia and transphobia of the people they protect, local police claimed an innocent victim to their witch hunt. Late at night on February 20th, someone whom the lead investigator later described as a middle aged transvestite was seen in Bitsa Park by police canvassing the area and whose mere presence was immediately deemed suspicious.

Accounts of what followed vary greatly, with many sources glossing over the resulting exchange entirely. Claims range from the suspect attempting to flee, mysteriously breaking free of handcuffs, to pulling a knife that was never found and threatening the policemen directly. One source described nearly 200 officers being called to the scene to detain this one person. The most agreed upon and substantiated elements of that night seem to be that the suspect had a hammer in their bag, and one thing led to another that resulted in police shooting the suspect in the leg and requiring hospitalization. It was later found that their "suspect" had corroborated, air-tight alibis for each of the murders and had done nothing wrong; the hammer had been for protection against the Maniac.

Apprehending the *Culprit*

Two months and nine bodies later, the police finally caught their break in the form of Marina Moskalyeva, the first victim since young Mikhail with direct ties to Pichushkin. Marina was a single mother to her 15 year old son and worked full time at the same grocery store as Sasha. Not only had they worked together, but when questioned after the fact, Marina's son described Pichushkin as her boyfriend and had met him before. Thanks to a subway ticket in the pocket of her jacket, police were able to easily find footage of Pichushkin meeting Marina at a metro station just outside Bitsa Park on the day of her murder. In case that had not been enough, Marina had left a note with her son saying she was going for a walk in the park, naming Sasha Pichushkin and even listing his phone number in case her son needed her.

Marina had known there was a killer at large in Bitsa Park and went anyway; likewise, Pichushkin knew Marina had left a note with his name and number, and still killed her. The man Marina knew—the shelf-stocker who lived with his mother, a man's man, a smoker and a drinker, her coworker—seemingly posed no threat. She had known him, trusted him enough to introduce him to her son. In the case of Pichushkin, investigators suggested that he craved the attention of getting caught, purposefully choosing a victim that would lead to his arrest. What seems more likely based on his confession, is that when given the opportunity to kill Sasha simply couldn't resist.

Within hours of being apprehended, Pichushkin confessed to not only Marina's murder and the twelve others the police are aware of, but claimed he had killed as many as 63 people. Plying him with sandwiches and cigarettes, detectives finally begin to understand the scope of the disappearances and consequent murders in and around the ignored *khrushchevki*. Following standard procedure for murder cases, Pichushkin is taken to the scene of the murders to reenact them on film, eventually to be used as evidence in his trial. Due to the extensiveness of his crimes, what is typically only a few hours of video continues on for nearly 40 hours filmed over the course of a month.

While Pichushkin's trial is much less of a spectacle than that of his idol, Chikatilo, it is still well publicized and attended by an aggravated crowd of his victims' families. Despite his fluctuating claims of 62 to 64 murders, the official charges brought to trial on September 13th are for 49 counts of murder and 3 attempted murders. Where police had ignored the voices of the lower class and their accounts of missing friends and families, the press steps in. With Sasha's quiet and undocumented past, journalists take statements from family members of victims, neighbors from Pichushkin's building, even random members of the community, stitching together a story for the Chessboard Killer, no matter how fabricated.

The most notable aspect of the trial was possibly the lack of controversy surrounding such a large and well-reported case. With very little deliberation, Pichushkin's psychological evaluation deemed him sane, stating that "his actions were purposeful and consistent... he was aware of what he was doing." After meeting for only three hours, the jury unanimously ruled Pichushkin guilty on all counts. Pichushkin's defense team filed an appeal within weeks but it was denied immediately. The first fifteen years of Pichushkin's life sentence were ordered to be spent in solitary confinement in a northern high security prison, where he remains today.

Despite the severity of his sentence, the prosecutors and the family of his victims are still divided in their opinions of his punishment. The chief prosecutor told the press immediately after the trial let out that he believed that "justice has been done... He received the punishment that he deserved." In contrast, Tamara Klimmova, whose husband fell victim to Pichushkin, demanded more.

"He should be handed over to the public for punishment rather than allowed to live in prison at our expense."

Now nearly nine years into his sentence, Pichushkin continues to serve out his punishment in solitary confinement. Sasha will be 44 years old when he integrates back into communal prison life, just another member of Russia's growing prison population of almost six hundred fifty thousand people, lost in the crowd of the criminal justice system.

SERIAL KILLING COP : THE TRUE STORY OF MIKHAIL POPKOV

FRANK COLEMAN

'He is charming and sociable. Women like him but he is a beast inside, and it is always hard to fight a werewolf.' - Mikhail Zavorin, police investigator

Mikhail Popkov may be the most prolific serial killers in world history.

He led a double-life as a family man with a wife and a young daughter. But after the dissolution of the Soviet Union, Popkov was able to take advantage of the lack of police authority to get away with his most barbaric fantasies.

Using his police uniform as a cover, he would lure unsuspecting women into his squad car where he would drive them to an isolated forest to kill them. His murders would go unabated for close to twenty years until Russian authorities finally utilized DNA evidence to match Popkov with the killings.

He was able to evade authorities because he was the authority.

Both he and his wife were police officers.

This is their story.

THE ORIGINS OF A KILLER

Mikhail Popkov was born on March 7th, 1964 in Russia. Little is known about his early life. He was a sporting youth like any other before entering the police academy. He would meet and marry Elene who was a fellow officer. The two would have a daughter, Ekaterina, who would later become a schoolteacher.

"I had a family," Popkov said. "My wife and daughter considered me a good husband and father, which corresponded to reality. I was in the service, in the police, having positive feedback on my work. I never thought of myself as mentally unhealthy. During my police service, I regularly passed medical commissions and was recognized as fit."

Accounts vary over what set off Popkov. His first known killing occurred in 1992 when he was twenty-eight years old. Most serial killers start showing anti-social behavior early in childhood. But Popkov is an anomaly in that there doesn't appear to be any early warning signs.

Popkov would claim that he never intended to become a serial killer and that it "just happened."

"I just felt I wanted to kill a woman I was give a lift to in my car," he said of his first victim in 1992.

The belief that his wife was having an affair with one of his co-workers, did seem to set him off course. His wife denied this claim vehemently but Popkov discovered two used condoms thrown in the garbage at his home. His wife claims that the condoms were used by some friends who were visiting for the night.

"I just had some reasons to suspect her," Popkov said. "I'm not looking for excuses, but this was the impetus for my future."

Fueled by a jealous rage, he began seeking out women that reminded him of his wife's sluttish ways.

Another theory is that he targeted women who reminded him of his mother. This is a typical Freudian response when assessing the motivation of serial killers who murder women...They are symbolically killing their mother.

In Popkov's case, however, this doesn't seem to hold weight. His mother would go on to the defend her son even when the evidence against him proved to be overwhelming. By all accounts, she seemed to have been a loving and doting mother to her "Mischa" as she called him.

THE ROUTINE

Popkov had an established modus operandi for abducting his victims. His targets would be women alone, often those who were drunk.

He would put on his police uniform and park his car outside discos and restaurants, waiting for a tipsy woman to come wobbling out. He would then lure her into his car with the promise of a ride.

"I could arrest you," Popkov would sometimes tell his victims. "But I'm feeling charitable. Get in and I'll take you home."

Other times, he would play the role of a cop looking out for a young woman's best interest.

"There have been reports of a man attacking women around here," he would tell the victim in a conspiratorial tone. "Let me take you home. We can't have you walking out on the streets alone."

Once inside his vehicle, however, Popkov would drive his trusting victim to an isolated forest. Once there he would force them to strip naked for him. He would become enraged, attacking them with whatever weapon he had on hand. Sometimes he used an axe, sometimes he used a knife while others he strangled to death. He would decapitate one of the victims and ripped out the heart of another.

"The choice of weapons for killing was always casual," Popkov said. "I never prepared beforehand to commit a murder. I would use any object that was in the car - a knife, an axe, a bat."

Then he would rape the victim post-mortem.

He would not go to great lengths to dump the body to avoid discovery. The attack would take place in an isolated area and he would leave bodies in the forest the side of the road and sometimes the cemetery.

Popkov nicknamed himself "The Cleaner", stating that it became his "misson" to rid the Russian streets of loose women.

"I had a double life," Popkov said. "In one life I was an ordinary person ... In my other life I committed murders, which I carefully concealed from everyone, realizing that this was a criminal offense."

"The victims were those who, unaccompanied by men, at night, without a certain purpose, were on the streets, behaving carelessly, who were not afraid to enter into conversation with me, get into my car, and then go for a drive in search of adventures, for the sake of entertainment, ready to drink alcohol and have sexual intercourse with me. Not all women became victims, but those of a certain negative behavior, I had a desire to teach and punish."

THE SOLE SURVIVOR

In 1998, he would attack a woman later referred to in the press as "Svetlana M."

Svetlana was fifteen but according to police looked older than her actual age.

She told investigators that a police car pulled up next to her and offered her a ride. Unsuspecting, she got into the vehicle where she was driven to a nearby forest.

Following his standard routine, Popkov ordered the girl to take off all her clothes. He then smashed her head against a tree and knocked her out.

He would violate her then leave her for dead.

The next day, Svetlana would be found, somehow still alive despite being completely naked in the sub-zero temperatures of the region.

She would awaken in the hospital and tell the police her story.

"She was unconscious because of severe head injuries," Nikolai Kitaev, one of the police investigators said. "Police did not start a criminal investigation for a long time despite numerous complaints from the girl's mother. Finally, Svetlana would be questioned and told in detail about her rapist-policeman and his car."

Police didn't believe her story. Svetlana, however, would identify Popkov as her attacker after she was shown a photograph of him in a police car. Police would question Popkov, who laughed it off. They also questioned his wife who stated that he was with her the whole night.

With an alibi by a trusted police officer let alone his wife, the police didn't pursue the matter any further.

"She (Svetlana) clearly confirmed it was him," Kitaev said. "But again, the police trusted Mikhail's wife - once more she composed an alibi for him and the criminal investigation was stopped and sent to the archives."

"It was enough just to perform a DNA test of this man but the police interrogated Popkov's wife who composed an alibi for her husband. Later he became more careful and carried on with his horrific crimes."

Knowing they had a serial killer/rapist on their hands, Russian investigators worked to construct a psychological profile of who their suspect could be. They surmised that he may be either a metalworker, bus driver, railroad worker or heating station engineer. They were also convinced that he may also have been a mortuary worker because so many bodies had been found at or near cemeteries.

Still, Popkov didn't have to do much to evade authorities. Russian investigators were still disorganized after the fall of the Soviet Union. He was able to elude and evade detection by simply being a little more organized than the people investigating him. It didn't take much, he knew their strengths and weaknesses...after all, he was one of them.

"There are two groups of maniacs - organized and non-organized," Russian psychiatrist Alexander Grishin said. "Non-organized maniacs are easy to catch, their crimes are quickly solved - they are people with psychiatric pathologies, who live in their own world, they are hiding from people, often untidy. Organized maniacs - Popkov is a good example - are people with high mental abilities, socially adapted, often with families, they find convenient jobs which secures them and gives time for crimes. It is a hard job to catch such a maniac, it is hard to spot such a person, even police enrollment tests are not good enough for it. The fact that only drunk women attracted him could be the result of his childhood problems and associations - his mother used to drink alcohol and often abused him. Maybe in his childhood other drunk women abused him too, and all this affected his behavior later in his adult life and led to such horrible consequences."

INCOMPETENCE LEADS TO MORE KILLINGS

The failure of the police authority to suspect Popkov coupled with his wife covering for him allowed him to murder several more women over the ensuing years.

One of those victims was Tanya Chagaeva, a 29-year old housewife with a daughter at home.

Tanya had received an invitation to go to a concert. Despite protestations from her husband who wanted her to stay home, Tanya wanted to take in the experience.

"It happened 15 year ago but the pain does not go away - it was me who presented Tanya a ticket to go to a concert, and she was killed after attending it', Viktoria Chagaeva, Tanya's sister said.

Her husband Igor was against his wife going to the concert but she would go anyway with her girlfriend, Yulia. The two would leave their home but not return.

Igor would call Viktoria in the morning, asking if his wife had gone to stay with her sister. They both then realized that Tanya was missing.

"I got truly scared," Viktoria said. "It was the first time, she had never done this before. There were no mobile phones at that time, we could only call Yulia's parents thinking Tanya must have stayed overnight there for some reason. But Yulia's parents said she had not come home either."

The police would prove to be of little help. They told the families that they would have to wait three days before the women could be qualified as a missing person.

Later that night, a farmer would find the naked bodies of both women in a village close to Angarsk.

"It was 1am when Tanya's husband Igor and I came to the police," Viktoria recalled. "We did not tell our mother yet. Igor was absolutely devastated and only repeated - 'She was killed, she was killed'. I was shocked too, but I simply could not believe it and replied - 'what are you talking about?' Later we were told that their bodies were found next to each other, both girls were raped, cut and chopped. The experts told us that at first they were killed then raped. My elder brother Oleg went to the morgue to identify Tanya. He had flown from Moscow immediately. He felt sick when saw the body, she was so mutilated. He was almost green when he came out of there - he just could not say a word. I did not dare to go in and look."

The police had already established the chain of events. Both Tanya and Yulia had left the concert and went out for a drink with some friends. Leaving the bar, they were then offered a ride by a policeman.

"Only the fact that this bastard was in a police uniform explains why Tanya got into his car," Viktoria said. "Many people attended Tanya's funeral. It felt as if the whole town was there. Our poor mother lost her consciousness several times, she needed a lot of medicine to cope. Igor was in almost the same condition. Tanya's coffin was open, her face was not hurt. He damaged the back of her skull, and her body was heavily cut. Yulia's coffin was closed, her face was cut up and disfigured."

Tanya's mother would never be the same.

"She felt as if she had died with Tanya, life became useless for her. She lived only because she was visiting various mediums one by one, looking for the killer and wasting her money. Nobody gave her any serious information but she kept doing it. She died in 2007 aged 66 from a heart attack. I think her heart could not cope with the pain any longer."

A REIGN OF TERROR

In August of 1999, Popkov would offer a medical student a ride. He would take her to the forest and chop off her head, stabbing her six times before stuffing down a garbage chute. Later that month he approached twenty-year old Maria Molotkova. Maria was leaving work from a water pumping station when Popkov offered her a ride. Maria was unsuspecting of the police officer, just like all the rest. He would drive her to the forest, kill then violate her corpse.

In June of 2000, he would claim two of his older victims, 35-year old Marina Lyzhina and 37-year old Lilia Pashkovskaya.

Marina and Lilia worked at the same shop and left to see Marina's sister. They worked late and started to walk home around midnight. They were going to call a taxi cab but changed their minds. The night was warm and they decided to walk.

Until Popkov came along in his police vehicle and picked the women up.

Popkov would murder the women but realize that he left his police badge behind at the scene.

"I found the token (badge) right away, but saw that one of the women was still breathing," Popkov said. "I was shocked by the fact that she was still alive. I finished her with a shovel."

The two women were buried in closed coffins. Their bodies had been so mutilated that the Russian tradition of having open coffins had to be disregarded. Marina had a 14-year old daughter. Lilia had two children, a 12-year old daughter and 3-year old son.

He then targeted a music teacher at his daughter's school.

"Her corpse was found in the forest along with the body of another woman," Popkov said. "My daughter asked me to give her money, because the school was collecting to organize funerals. I gave [it to] her."

Popkov then step down from his policemen duties. He would find work in the security business, working as a guard for the Angarsk Oil and Chemical company.

FALSE CLAIMS?

Popkov would claim that he stopped killing when he became impotent as he contracted syphilis from one of his victims. There is no word if he transferred the disease to his wife as well.

The press would dub him as "The Wednesday Murder" as that was the day his victims were typically found. One detective working on the case would refer to him as a "werewolf."

It is reported that he did not stop killing after he contracted the sexually transmitted disease. Investigators are still looking at murders from the time he worked as a traveling security guard.

ARREST

On June 23rd, 2012, Popkov would be arrested in Vladivostok when he was buying a car. He had his DNA sampled along with 3,500 other police officers and his sample was matched with the semen he left behind on his victims.

"I could not anticipate the examination of DNA," Popkov said to investigators. "I was born in another century. Now there are such modern technologies, methods, but not earlier. If we have not got to that level of genetic examination, then ... I would not be sitting in front of you."

After Popkov's identity was revealed to the press, Tanya Chagaeva's sister Viktoria realized that she knew the man.

They had both competed in a biathlon at the same gym.

"I was stuck with horror when I saw the picture of this maniac in the paper and online," Viktoria said. "My sister's killer was looking into my eyes. I immediately felt as if I'd met him. Looking at him, I could hardly breathe. Some minutes later I looked at him another time and thought - oh my God, I know him! I was so shocked, I even took a knife and cut his face in the newspaper, I needed to let this horror out of me. I remember him as a tall slim man, he was always alone, with a slippery and shifty glance. I think such people just must not live. This beast took the life of my sister, who had so many happy years in front of her. I cried a lot that day, but it is time to be quiet and just wait. He will be punished by law and criminals in jail will punish him too, I am sure he will pay for all the murders one day...."

His fellow police officers who worked with him were shocked as well.

"When I read about him in the press I literally choked," said Dmitry Valuev. "Because I used to work with him and thought I knew him. He was an absolutely normal man. He liked biathlon; once on duty he shot a rapist during an arrest. There was an investigation and he was not punished, the chiefs considered he had taken fair action."

"I used to work closely with him for 5 years," Sergey Golovkin said. "He knew lots of jokes and stories, and could be soul of the party."

His own daughter was shocked. To this day, she does not believe that her father committed those murders

"I do not believe any of this," Ekaterina said. "I always felt myself as 'Daddy's girl'. For 25 years we were together, hand in hand. We walked, rode bikes, went to the shops, and he met me from school. We both collect model cars, so we have the same hobby.

"I wanted to be a criminologist, so I read a book with tips of how investigators catch serial killers and there were also basic classifications [about murderers]. Daddy doesn't fit any of these classifications - he doesn't look like some maniac."

But Ekaterina recently changed her tone, not having seen her father for over two years. She expressed a desire to "look into his eyes and understand if he really could be that killer"

Popkov's wife continues to support him although she no longer offers alibis. She would describe the charges against the husband as "fairy tales".

"We met on the Monday and Tuesday before sentencing and discussed this situation," Elena Popkov said. "He already knew that it would be a life sentence. He denied everything. Even when our daughter Katya asked him, he said, 'Katya, you understand that all these [allegations] are fairy tales. It is the system - I have worked within it, I know this system well. We have been married for 28 years. If I suspected something wrong, of course, I would divorce with him. I support him, I believe him. If he were to be released right now, I would not say a word and we would continue to live together. I love him, I support him. He did not cause me any harm for all these years. I felt safe with him."

Elena would not be the only woman to step up and defend Popkov. His mother would address the press as well and express her support.

"I cannot believe he walked alone to the forest in a police uniform," Popkov's mother said. "Where was the blood? His clothes should have been covered in blood or if he had tried to wash the blood away, the clothes would have been wet. His wife would definitely have noticed all that. He loves his family, cherishes his daughter, and he dreamed about grandchildren. He would not have done this. He will remain my son, until my death. He studied well and from the very beginning he was excellent pupil. He loved to cook, pancakes or something like this and he was very neat, like me."

But even his own mother had her doubts...

"Misha (Mikhail), give us some sign if you have done all this or not. And if so, why? It is hard to live knowing nothing. We need to know."

Popkov was initially suspected of killing twenty-nine women. Twenty-five of the women were aged 19 to 28 while four were between the ages of 35 to 40. All victims lived in Angarsk, Irkutsk.

Later, however, the Russian authorities admitted that the numbers were considerably higher after they interrogated Popkov.

"To clarify the numbers, Popkov has confessed to 59 new murders," Irkutsk Investigative Committee spokeswoman Karina Golovacheva said. "We are not counting in this total those 22 for which he was already sentenced. These cases are already closed. So there are 59 new murders. That means, if we add them to the earlier 22, it will be 81 murders in total."

Popkov would charged with an additional forty-seven murders with another twelve still pending.

"We are quite sure about the 12 other cases," Golovacheva said. "We are now gathering all the evidence. Further analysis of the evidence is underway and 'in the nearest future we can bring charges in these 12 cases' which Popkov has already admitted"

Based on Popkov's confession it appears that he is the most prolific serial killer in Russia history. He has a higher kill count that Andrei Chikatilo, aka the Butcher of Rostov, who had been convicted of over fifty-three murders. Alexander Pichushkin and Anatoly Onoprienko were convicted of fifty-two and forty-nine respectively.

But authorities now believe that he is "rationing out his confessions" as he is delaying his time in the Russian jail system before being sentenced to serve out the rest of his life in a brutal penal colony where he will be forced into hard labor.

Because he traveled so much after leaving his police job, authorities believe that Popkov is responsible for even more murders than already suspected.

THE MAD RUSSIAN KILLER : THE TRUE STORY OF SERGEY GOLOVKIN

Before the fall of the Berlin Wall and the ultimate demise of the Soviet Union, little was known about the crimes that were committed behind the iron curtain. The law enforcement did their best to keep the information from the western media and paint a picture of a perfect society where murder do not happen. However, one serial killer managed to keep thousands of people on their toes back in 1980s and 1990s. He was known as the Fisher or Boa, and his hunting ground was Odinstovo district which is located in the general Moscow area.

The sadistic way of killing and the very fact that he targeted little boys was enough to scare everyone living in that part of the Soviet Union. Fisher's identity was unknown for years and he reached the status of an unpredictable killer who was always one step ahead of the police. But detectives worked really hard on this case and eventually identified him as Sergey Golovkin. So let's take a closer look at one of the most notorious killers from the Eastern Europe who roamed free for six years before he was finally brought to justice.

Golovkin's early life

Sergey Golovkin was born on November 26th, 1959 in Moscow. He had a standard working class upbringing which was quite usual in the Soviet Russia. Sergey's mother had a regular job, while his father suffered from alcoholism and had a bad temper. He didn't stand out as a child and suffered from various illnesses, making him appear a bit odd to his peers. He often had bronchitis, intestinal problems, and urinary infections. It is possible that the fact Sergey was often recovering from various diseases contributed to his shyness and the inability to connect with the other children. Even when Golovkin was feeling better, he kept to himself and played on his own.

His upbringing was quite strict and his father would often try to cure his son by pouring cold water on his head in order to make him more resistant to the sickness. Sergey hated these treatments and started avoiding water and showering altogether. It was another reason why his peers and neighbors stayed away from him. The relationship with his parents was pretty cold and young Golovkin didn't get all the love he probably craved back then.

Even though he was quiet by nature, Sergey was a solid student. He had good grades and some moderate academic success in middle and high school. However, he was still a loner and seemed not to have any notable hobbies that would help him get noticed. Teenagers can be pretty cruel and it seems like Sergey was often a target for the bullies, mostly because of his physical appearance. Classmates would later describe him as tall and awkward with a face covered with pimples. Another thing that puzzled his high-school friends was the fact that Sergey never showed interest in any of the girls and he was never seen with an actual girlfriend.

After finishing high-school, Sergey continued his education at Timiryazev Agricultural Academy. He was interested in that field of study and maintained solid grades until his graduation in 1982. But the time he spent at the academy was also very stressful to Sergey. He was often targeted by local hooligans and gangs who lived nearby. It was a common thing in Soviet Russia back in 1980s and the gang-related crimes were on the rise. However, these vicious attacks helped Sergey to develop and refine his own twisted fantasies and set him up on a path to becoming a sadistic killer in the future. He started relating aggression to sex and he would often masturbate after the beatings. He plotted out the revenge against his attackers and it often included rape and torture.

It was clear that Sergey started developing the first signs of the sadistic behavior back then. He also had an image of his perfect victim deep in his mind that would emerge every time he was aroused. His ideal target would be a boy who is less than fifteen years old, with thin physique and jet black hair. Fresh out of agricultural academy, Sergey needed to find a job. He became a horse-breeding expert at an institute which was located on the outskirts of Moscow.

Sergey did turn out to be quite handsome and his puberty acne did clear up, but he was still reserved and kept to himself. But his fantasies were getting more and more serious, running through his mind all the time, and they were about to escalate in a very violent way.

The first attack

In the summer of 1984, Golovkin committed his first offense. The attack happened in a camp and it was not planned at all. Golovkin was sitting near a fence, smoking a cigarette, when a very young boy approached him. Golovkin himself would talk about the incident later and testify that he had no idea how the attack happened. He claimed that his mind became blurry and he was completely disoriented but aware of the boy and the knife in his hand. His young victim was stabbed numerous times and his face was covered with a cloth afterwards. Golovkin fled the scene, running away from the camp towards the wooded area. Even though the scene of crime looked very brutal, the boy did not have any life-threatening wounds and he would survive the attack. It is also important to mention that Golovkin tried to strangle the boy as well, leaving him with visible marks around his neck. Police wasn't sure what was used around the boy's neck, but Golovkin would confirm that he tried to strangle his first victim with a rope.

The boy recovered from this attack and would later testify against Golovkin in 1993. He became one of the key witnesses and seemed to recall that hot summer day in 1984 perfectly clear. It was obvious that this attack happened suddenly and that Golovkin himself wasn't prepared for it. His murder fantasies simply took over him and the very fact that he was inexperienced probably saved this boy's life. Unfortunately, Golovkin would take this incident as a lesson and use it in order to establish his new modus operandi which would turn him into one of the most prolific murderers in the history of Soviet Russia.

The police did investigate this incident and did their best to find out as much as they could about the perpetrator. The boy did give them a description but the investigators weren't able to match it to anyone. There were no other witnesses who saw what happened on that day in camp and eventually, this case was forgotten. There were no new leads and the files would end up collecting dust until the 1990s. On the other hand, Golovkin would not make the same mistake again. He knew that killing his victims was the only way to make sure he would not be identified by any of them. It was just a matter of time when he would get another opportunity to kill.

The emergence of Fisher

The cooling down period lasted a couple of years for Golovkin. He was worried that he might be identified right after the attack, but as the time went on, he realized that the police had nothing on him. His sadistic thoughts and needs were slowly becoming more violent and he felt that he had to find another victim.

On the evening of April 19th 1986, Golovkin was walking from the train station in Katuar Dmitrov district of Moscow when he spotted a sixteen years old boy riding his bicycle. His name was Andrey Pavlov and he was returning home from a visit to his grandparents. Andrey was supposed to check the birch sap containers his father placed on nearby trees and bring them back home. This task included biking through a secluded area. Golovkin followed him and when to boy jumped off his bike to take a short break, he approached him and asked for matches. It was a perfect opportunity for Golovkin because there was no one in sight.

When Andrey failed to return home that evening, his father decided to look for him. He knew the boy's typical route and though that he might have fallen off the bike and hurt himself. Unfortunately, Andrey's father found his boy tied up by the path. The scene looked like something out of a horror movie. When the investigators arrived, they discovered that the boy was bound, raped, and tortured. His genitals were cut off and there were signs of strangulation. Andrey was also stabbed and his throat was slashed. The further examination of the crime scene revealed numerous fingerprints on the bike but none of them belonged to Golovkin.

The detectives interviewed the locals and some of them did report seeing a tall man with dark hair with visible pimples on his face. They were sure he wasn't from their village, but the description itself didn't help the investigators right away. They did manage to create a solid sketch but still had no suspect.

As the summer of 1986 approached, Golovkin was already searching for his next victim. He remembered his first murder attempt which happened in a camp and started running through different possible scenarios. Since the school break was here, camps will be at their full capacity, and they will be a perfect place to find his next victim. It was common for parents to send their children away during the summer in almost all Eastern bloc countries. However, one camp will become a scene of a grisly murder.

It seemed like the authorities completely forgot about Golovkin's first attempted murder and the camps in the area didn't have any additional security on the premises. The counselors did notice a younger man who would stand around and observe the children but they didn't pay too much attention to him. Nobody could predict the tragedy which will occur shortly after.

On July 12th 1986, a twelve-year-old boy disappeared from a camp called "Star" which was located in Odintsovo district. The counselors immediately sent out a couple of search parties to the nearby woods and one of them stumbled upon a brutal crime scene. The boy's body was in horrible condition and it was obvious to everyone that whoever did this was a deeply disturbed killer.

The investigators concluded that the boy was raped, strangled, and hanged from a tree. His genitals were removed and the stomach was cut with precision. The detectives were now certain that they were looking for someone who had medical knowledge and was familiar with the anatomy. His head was missing from the crime scene and the wound on the neck indicated that it was removed cleanly with a sharp object. There were dozens of stab wounds on his body. The head was later found near a path that led out of the woods, meaning that the killer must have carried it away with him, and suddenly decided to throw it away.

The detectives immediately linked this crime to the murder of Andrey Pavlov because there were so many similarities between them. It was clear that they were dealing with a serial murderer who targeted young boys and acted alone, carefully planning each and every step. Sergey Golovkin did appear at this crime scene once the body was discovered and he stood in the background. Some of the locals did notice him, but couldn't provide the officers with a good description because he was constantly turning his head away from them.

Soon enough, police did find a witness. It was one of the boys from the camp who claimed that he saw his friend with an older man who had a distinctive tattoo on his arm. The boy testified that the man's tattoo design included a snake and the word 'Fisher'. The boy continued to add various details to his testimony and some detectives doubted his story. However, they had to check every lead.

The police didn't know if Fisher was a surname, nickname, or name so they ended up questioning everyone who had any connection to this phrase. The boy also provided them with a sketch so that made the investigation slightly easier. Unfortunately, the boy's testimony was a product of overactive imagination and it would sidetrack the police investigation for years because they were focused on finding a perpetrator that fit this description. On the other hand, the maniac who terrorized the Moscow area finally had a name – the Fisher. The public will give him another nickname soon after and he would also be known as Boa.

The basement of horrors

While police worked really hard in order to follow every single lead they had, Sergey Golovkin continued living his life comfortably. He was very confident that the authorities will not link him to either of the murders. He was in his cooling off period, but the stories of the Fisher continued to scare the citizens of Moscow and the surrounding rural areas. Parents took the threat seriously and didn't let their children out of sight. Summer camps were supervised better and everyone was on a constant lookout. Police did receive a large number of possible suspects and they did continue their investigation. There were no new bodies and the public relaxed a bit.

Golovkin bought a car in 1988 which made him more mobile and there was no need for him to stalk his victims in the woods anymore. It was a beige Lada 1500 and he would use it to commit his next murder in 1989. The car itself was a generic working class car that didn't stand out in any way. It would help Golovkin blend in easily and avoid getting caught.

The acquisition of the brand new vehicle prompted Golovkin to build a garage and modify it even further. He started digging a small cellar area which was supposed to be his workshop. As he was working on his new basement, he realized that this space would be ideal for torturing his victims. The basement layout changed quickly because Golovkin added the full concrete floor, rings on the walls and ceiling, etc. He made sure the lighting was perfect and the powerful bulbs illuminated the basement. He created his own little personal den where he could do whatever he wanted to without the fear of being caught red handed.

Golovkin evolved as a murderer as well. After kidnapping a boy from a bus station back in 1989, and seeing how many people were involved in the search for him, Golovkin decided to prey on young runaways and delinquents who were forgotten by their families. Nobody would notice that they were missing right away and that gave him enough time to keep them in his basement.

The car became a very powerful tool and Golovkin would go searching for his new victims as soon as he got back home from work. He would drive around the surrounding neighborhoods, watching the young men who loitered on the streets by using binoculars. He looked for boys who were smoking and looked a bit unkempt. This was his signal that the parents were not particularly involved in their son's life. Once he selected his next victim, he would befriend the boy and eventually invite him into his car.

Even though Golovkin was socially awkward, he did manage to strike up a conversation with these teenagers. He would often ask for a match or a lighter which was a good opening line. Golovkin justified his murders by claiming that these teenagers were criminals who were robbing houses, drinking, and fighting. But it was clear that he was reliving his fantasy because the said teenagers reminded him of his own childhood bullies and they had to pay for everything they have done to him when he was young.

The body of a boy who was kidnapped in September of 1989 was discovered in 1990. He was in a bad state of decomposition and his remains were scattered over a large wooded area. Even though animals did consume the majority of his corpse, it was obvious that the boy was tortured and skinned alive. The familiar marks were there – signs of sadism, strangulation marks around his neck, removal of the genitals, and a large number of stab wounds. It was surprising how long it took the authorities to find this boy because the initial search was large and included police squads from various parts of Moscow.

Golovkin will later tell everything that happened after the boy's disappearance. He took him to his garage, raped him while holding a knife to his throat, hung the boy from the ceiling, and eventually strangled him. He took his time with the corpse, removing the skin carefully and leaving the remains in a less populated area. He kept the head in his garage, cleaned it up, and used it to frighten his future victims.

Police were now sure that they are dealing with a killer who has a surgical knowledge and they started combing through the nearby hospitals, as well as any establishment that worked with surgical instruments. Golovkin's place of employment was also searched but everyone who worked there was certain that they didn't have a sadistic killer in their ranks and that the authorities were making a mistake.

Golovkin continued his murderous spree completely unbothered by the fact that the police was investigating the horse-breeding institute he worked at. Another boy disappeared in August of 1990. He was supposed to travel to Vlasikha which is a military town. Two more boys disappeared in October of the same year. They were students in a local high school and their parents notified the authorities right away. Unfortunately, their dismembered bodies will be found next year.

Police closing in

In 1991, Russia was going through a huge political turmoil. Moscow was flooded with military and police – the entire area was locked in because the authorities were concerned about the safety of the now former president of the Soviet Union Mikhail Gorbachev. But regardless of the heightened security measures, Golovkin kidnapped and murdered another victim in that time. Since Moscow was in the full lockdown, this crime was essential in determining the location of the man they were hunting.

Nobody was able to go in or out the Moscow area and the barricades separated different parts of the city. They knew where the boy was last seen and police used this information to estimate Fisher's place of residence. They also knew that the man they were looking for had a vehicle and a place to hide. If he attempted to murder the boy on the street, a soldier or a police officer would very likely see him because they were everywhere. This very fact shortened the list of suspects significantly.

Another clue was the salt on the boy's skin. It was clear that a large amount of this substance was used in order to dry out the corpse and not everyone was able to get it back then. It was industrial salt which can usually be found on farms. The authorities also suspected that the perpetrator removed a couple of muscles from the body, possibly in order to eat them. They checked various mental institutions in and around Moscow, but no patient fitted the profile. The investigators visited the horse breeding institute for the second time in order to see if they were missing large amounts of industrial salt.

Since they also had a general description of the suspect, the police tried to find a dark haired, tall and lanky male in his thirties. Only one employee resembled their sketches and that was Sergey Golovkin. They haven't questioned him so far because he wasn't registered as the resident of that area and somehow managed to avoid the list of possible suspects.

In the meantime, three more boys disappeared from the area. They were friends who often went to an amusement park in Moscow together. The boys lived near the horse breeding institute and were last seen with Sergey Golovkin. The man was their acquaintance and they liked hanging out with him because he would often talk about horses. Detectives arrested Golovkin two weeks after the mushroom pickers discovered the bodies in the woods. Golovkin broke down and told them everything, leading the police to the place of the burial, and describing everything that happened.

Police searched Golovkin's garage and basement, finding the crucial evidence in a small bathtub which was used for draining the blood of his victims. The rest of the basement was kept in pristine condition while the tub contained traces of skin, teeth, and other DNA. They also found a diverse collection of knives. A large number of them were surgical knives and high quality blades that allowed Golovkin to stab and dissect his victims with precision.

The lawyer that took over this case in 1992 was Vladimir Ilyich Kolesnikov who had a good reputation among his colleagues. He knew how to catch and detain the most notorious killers. Kolesnikov had an eye for details and he connected the dots quickly. Sergey Golovkin was off the streets and they knew they had the right man. With eleven confirmed victims (and two or more who were still being investigated),

Golovkin was waiting for his trial. Children and parents who lived in Moscow could relax because Fisher was finally caught.

The trial and sentence

The trial itself wasn't open for public. The prosecution had a solid case and Golovkin's confession which was more than enough. However, the defense did play the insanity card. The psychiatrist determined that Golovkin was in fact completely sane and that he was aware of his deeds. He planned ahead and knew how to hide the evidence. But the psychiatrist did state that he showed some minor signs of schizophrenia.

The independent psychiatrist who worked with the police and was the one who made the initial profile did examine the findings that were presented in court and had a lot to say about Golovkin's mental state and the direct connection it has with the sexuality: "Sexual murders have the common characteristics which are always associated with the intimate life of the perpetrator, his traumatic sexual experiences, his sense of his sexual failure, inferiority, and those facts will allow you to call these murders intimate. In short, almost all serial sexual murderers were sexual failures or perceived themselves as such."

It was evident that Sergey Golovkin was a pedophile, a sadist, and a murderer. He killed and tortured his young victims in the most vicious ways imaginable. The underlying issues that plagued him from the early childhood probably did emerge from his tough upbringing. He was a weak child who was often bullied by his peers. Golovkin's parents believed in tough love and tried to make their boy stronger by using methods that might be called very cruel in our day and age.

Golovkin's childhood friends were also brought to the court, testifying against him. Some of them said that Golovkin was particularly cruel to animals when he was younger and would often kill and skin them. His former friends also claimed that Golovkin showed early signs of voyeurism and would often watch people bathing in a nearby river.

The defense was strongly against the death penalty in this case, citing that the reason behind their client's acts was dysfunctional upbringing and that his actions were a result of a violent and difficult childhood. The prosecution was set on winning and they knew that life in prison would not be enough for the families of the victims

Ultimately, Golovkin was found guilty of murdering and raping eleven boys. The investigators knew that there were at least thirteen victims but were unable to make Golovkin talk about the remaining two boys. There were also charges of theft and burglary. Regional Court in Moscow delivered the death sentence on October 19th 1994.

Golovkin would spend two years in prison, waiting for his execution. He would often read spiritual books and keep to himself, claiming that he found peace in religion. His mother visited him in prison regularly.

The death penalty was carried out on August 2nd 1996, bringing closure to everyone involved with this case. Golovkin was the last executed prisoner in Russia before this country abolished the death penalty.

THE SUMNERS

DINA LIVINGSTONE

When James "Reggie" and Carol Sumner moved to Jacksonville, Florida for their retirement, they had visions of good health and happiness. They never thought that their overnight invitation to long-time South Carolina neighbor, Tiffany Cole, would end up the way it did; With the Sumner couple being buried alive.

Reggie and Carol Sumner were high school sweethearts in North Charleston, South Carolina. They were the kind of couple that everyone envied as they walked down the hall. Unfortunately, their lives pulled them in different directions. Reggie decided to serve his country in the navy. After finishing his tour, he got married and landed a job with the railroad. Carol also married and became a devoted mother, however, her first marriage ended in divorce, and her second nearly killed her. In 1987, after years of abuse, her husband at the time shot her seven times in their home before driving away and turning the gun on himself. Her daughter, Rhonda Alford, just ten years old at that time, spent almost a year helping her mother recover from her wounds. She had to help her bathe, dress, and take care of the house. After taking eight years to fully recover, Carol went back to work as soon as she was able. For over twenty-five years she was a civil servant at the Citadel and the Charleston Air Force Base. She also worked a second job at night at a Belk department store, among other jobs she would take when needed. She did whatever she had to in order to make ends meet. Shortly after her recovery, she found out that the blood transfusion she had received during her previous trauma had given her Hepatitis C. She was angry because she felt as though she could not escape her late ex-husband, but she refused to let it ruin her life. She soon started a new job at a cable company and it was during this time that her life finally changed for the better. Nearly forty years after they'd left high school, a chance encounter brought Carol and Reggie together again. One night in 2000, a phone call was made to the cable company where Carol was working, which she received. After talking with the customer Carol and learning his name, she realized that he also sounded just like the Reggie she remembered. So she asked him if he was the same Reggie Sumner who attended Garrett High school in South Charleston. It was. They decided that they should get together after not seeing each other in so long. This time, though they were inseparable. Like "teenagers in love", a quick courtship led to love and then marriage in 2001 with a ceremony at Carol's home in West Ashley. Carol's daughter has said of Reggie "he was just a very gentle, kind and giving spirit. You could not ask for a better friend, husband or stepfather." Eventually, after retiring, the couple decided to move from South Carolina to Jacksonville, Florida. Reggie had previously bought a house during his days working for CSX railroad and as he was a "brittle" diabetic in frail health, he thought he would be more comfortable in the warmer climate. Carol agreed. "She only went down there to honor her husband," Rhonda said. Before moving, they decided to sell their Chevrolet Lumina to the stepdaughter of a friend who lived down the street, Tiffany Cole. They allowed her to make payments on the car to help her out and she agreed, often driving down to Jacksonville with friends to make those payments. Tiffany and the Sumners became friends and Tiffany would often spend the night at their house when she and her friends went down south. A pleasant girl on the outside, the Sumners had no idea what Tiffany could really be like.

Tiffany Ann Cole was born on December 3, 1981, to her sixteen-year-old mother, Shirley Duncan. Her biological father was in jail. She had no male role model to look up to or who could offer her protection the way a father should. Her mother had a boyfriend, but he was beyond cruel and especially loved to torment Tiffany. At one point, she had a puppy which her stepdad threw against a wall, breaking its neck right in front of her. He was abusive verbally as well as physically and Tiffany claims that as a young girl, he began to molest her, beginning around age eight. As a young teenager, she turned to alcohol and drugs to deal with the pain. In high school, Tiffany was a student who participated in cheerleading and played the flute. She was also a girl scout member but eventually the alcohol and drugs took over her life and she quit her programs and dropped out of school. At one point she fell in love with a boy with severe epilepsy, who ended up breaking her heart and since the only example of love from a man came from an abusive stepfather, this breakup reinforced the belief that she should expect to be treated badly and let down by men. She began looking for love in all the wrong places. In May of 2005, during a six-month period of prostitution, Tiffany ran into a man by the name of Michael Jackson. They were drawn to each other right away and began to get high and sleep together.

Michael James Jackson, born May 12, 1982, had a significant criminal history beginning in childhood. Born to a drug-addicted mother, he was mostly raised by his grandmother. He had multiple felony convictions but only for things like fraud and theft. After meeting Tiffany and becoming close, they took a road trip, first going to Myrtle Beach, then driving to Jacksonville, Florida, where they would be staying with Michael's best friend, Alan Wade. Born May 22, 1987, Alan and Michael had known each other for just over a year. When Tiffany and Michael arrived in Florida, they stayed at Alan's mom's house. After just a few days, though, she kicked them out because she was tired of the loud noises and constant partying. With nowhere else to go and with all their money spent on the nights of drinking and partying, Tiffany remembered that the Sumners lived nearby. The three friends showed up at their doorstep and explained what had happened. The couple was very happy to see Tiffany and invited her and her friends to stay the night. While they were chatting and catching up, Carol mentioned how worried they had been about their house in North Carolina not selling. There was no need to worry, however, because not only did their property sell, but they had also made a $99,000 profit. It was this general statement to a long-time neighbor that sealed the Sumner's fate.

It's difficult to know just whose idea it was to rob the Sumner's. Some say it was both Tiffany and Michael, while others say it was Michael who was the plan maker and master manipulator. Either way, a plan was hatched to rob and kill the loving couple. At some point in June, Alan had contacted his friend, Bruce Nixon Jr., and told him of a plan to rob someone. No other details were given. Then on July 6th, Alan called Bruce, born May 9th, 1987, and asked him if he would be interested in joining the others in digging a hole. Bruce agreed and stole four shovels from his neighborhood. The other three friends drove to Bruce's house in a rented Mazda RX-8 that Tiffany had rented in South Carolina. The group drove around hoping to find a perfectly remote place for the hole to be dug. Alan asked Bruce if he knew of any good places to which Bruce responded that he did. He took them into Georgia, to a wooded area just over the state line. Leaving the car parked on the road, the group walked through the wooded area into a clearing where they began to dig a hole while Tiffany held a flashlight. It was approximately four feet deep and six feet square. Upon completion of the hole, they left the shovels and went back to the car. It was here that Alan asked Michael if Bruce could join in on their robbery plan. Michael agreed. The foursome drove back to Alan's house but his mother would not allow Michael in as she believed him to be a bad influence on her son. Over the next couple of days, it was Tiffany's job to remain in contact with Carol and Reggie in order to gain information from them about their plans and whereabouts. The foursome also secretly watched the house in order to figure out the Sumner's routine. It was unclear yet as to whether or not the group would enter the home while the couple was gone or if they would simply go in with the couple there. It was ultimately decided that they would enter the home while the couple was there so that they could get their financial information and the means to access their accounts. Michael said that he would kill the victims by injecting them with a lethal dose of their medications. He then promised that the four friends would split the money they received from the Sumner's accounts, each receiving about $50,000. They began making preparations for their plan. Just after midnight on July 8th, 2005, Michael, Tiffany, and Alan went to Wal-Mart and purchased disposable rubber gloves. On the evening of the murders, they went to an Office Depot, where Tiffany bought duct tape and a large roll of plastic wrap. Last, they bought a toy gun that shot plastic pellets.

Around 10pm., on July 8th, 2005, Tiffany drove the other three group members to the Sumner's house in the Mazda. Herself and Michael remained in the car while Alan and Bruce went up to the door. They had the duct tape and toy gun and both were wearing the plastic gloves. After Carol answered the door, Bruce and Alan told her that they were having car trouble and asked if they could use their phone. Carol said of course they could and invited them in. As soon as the boys entered the home, Alan pulled the phone cord out of the wall. Bruce pointed the gun at the couple. Alan grabbed Reggie around the neck and pushed him down into a chair. They told the couple that they wanted credit and debit cards and any other financial information. Carol began pleading with the boys not to hurt them. Bruce took the couple into a spare bedroom where he used duct tape to bind their legs and hands and to cover their mouths and eyes. Alan sent a text message to Michael, informing him that everything was under control. Michael then also entered the home and he and Alan began searching for financial information. They saw a pile of mail and financial statements which they put into a plastic bag. They spotted Reggie's prized coin collection and took that too. Michael told the other two to take the couple into the garage at which point they put them into the trunk of the Lincoln Town car. Tiffany went into the house and grabbed some of their belongings, put them into a bag and took the bag with her to the Mazda. Following the plan, both cars headed towards the gravesite, stopping only once to put gas in the Lincoln. Upon arrival at the site, Michael opened the trunk and apparently began screaming when he saw that the duct tape had become loose and the couple had worked the tape off. It had been over 100 degrees in the trunk. Sweat had caused the tape to loosen. They had also taken the tape off their eyes and were huddled together. Michael ordered Bruce to tape them up again, which he did. Alan then attempted to back up the car to the edge of the grave but, unable to do so, Bruce took over. Michael then sent Bruce up the road to wait with Tiffany at the Mazda. While still alive, the Sumners were taken out of the trunk and pushed into the hole. It is unclear as to who actually did the burying because Alan and Michael each blamed the other. Somehow, Michael ended up getting the personal identification number of the Sumner's bank account. Reports differ on whether he obtained this information from somewhere in the house or if Carol told him the number while being threatened to be buried alive. According to one documentary, Carol had gotten the tape off her mouth again when in the hole. Michael was telling them that if they didn't give up their PIN, they would die, at which point Carol yelled it out. It didn't seem to matter either way though because they continued to shovel dirt onto the scared couple.

After filling the hole, Alan and Michael put the shovels back into the trunk of the Lincoln and drove it up the road to where Tiffany and Bruce were waiting with the Mazda. The four of them drove to Sanderson, Florida, where they abandoned the Lincoln after wiping it clean of fingerprints. They then drove back to Jacksonville where they immediately went to an ATM and withdrew money from the Sumner's account, before retiring to a hotel. Alan and Tiffany went to another Wal-Mart where they purchased more latex gloves as well as bleach. They returned to the Sumner's home in order to clean up any evidence. They also stole a computer. Bruce stayed with the group for another day and then went home, but Alan remained with Michael and Tiffany who returned to South Carolina, where Tiffany rented two hotel rooms; one for herself and Michael and one for Alan. It should be noted that after returning home, Bruce went to a party with a plastic bag filled with different medications. At one point he announced that he had found a new job murdering people. He stated that he had buried people alive and killed them without mentioning the involvement of anyone else.

On the morning of July 10th, Carol's daughter, Rhonda, decided to report to police the fact that she hadn't been able to get hold of her mother for a few days. Since they kept in touch on a regular basis and spoke every couple days, it was highly unusual for her mother to not return her calls. The next day, the Jacksonville Sheriff's Office (JSO) went to the Sumner's home. The back door of the house was unlocked and in the kitchen there dirty after-dinner plates, which was also highly unusual for the couple. The JSO began to investigate the financial accounts of the couple and they found that large amounts of money had been withdrawn within a short time frame. Video footage from the ATM machines that the group had used showed Michael's face and the silver Mazda in the background. On July 12th, after Rhonda made a plea on local TV networks for the safe return of her parents, the Sheriff's office received a phone call from someone posing as Reggie Sumner. Dispatch contacted Detective David Meacham of the Sheriff's office and put the caller through.

Meacham: Where are you at?

Michael: We're in Delaware right now

Meacham: And what city is that in?

Michael: It's in Corpus

Meacham: Corpus, Delaware?

Michael: Yes

However, the town of Corpus, Delaware does not exist. Next, Tiffany came on the phone posing as Carol.

Meacham: Is this Carol?

Tiffany: Yes, sir, it is.

Meacham: Okay. This is Detective Meacham from the Sheriff's office. How are you doing tonight?

Tiffany: I was sleeping

Meacham: I understand. I understand you have some health problems

Tiffany: Mmhmm

Meacham: Okay. Any other problems?

Tiffany: I'm really tired right now

Meacham: What kind of problems do you have?

Tiffany: Cancer

Meacham: Cancer?

Tiffany: Mmhmm

The detective called Rhonda into the station so that she could listen to the taped conversation. She confirmed that the people posing as the Sumners were definitely not Carol and Reggie. The main reason for the call was to ensure everyone that the Sumners were alive and well and because the bank accounts had been frozen. They asked the detectives to reinstate the accounts, which they did so that they could track the money in order to locate the perpetrators. They also had the phone number from which Michael had called. Using this information, they were able to find that the phone was registered to Michael and that a call had been placed to a car rental agency in Charleston. They also learned that the cell had been used near the Sumner's home the night of the murders. Detective Meacham contacted the rental company and was told that the car had been rented to a Tiffany Cole and that it was overdue. Using the rental car's GPS system, they were able to find that the car had also been near the Sumner's residence during the time of the abduction. Using the cell phone trace, the car's GPS and the photos of Michael at different ATMs, police were able to locate the general whereabouts of the three murderers. On July 14th, with help from Tiffany's brother, who was on probation and threatened with jail, police raided a Best Western hotel in Charleston and arrested Tiffany

Cole, Alan Wade, and Michael Jackson. Bruce Nixon was also picked up at his home in Florida.

While Tiffany, Michael, and Alan refused to cooperate with law enforcement, Bruce appeared to have some semblance of a conscience because he broke down and admitted to the crimes right away. He also agreed to lead police to the burial site. For the first time in TV history, documentary footage showed Bruce and detectives at the grave site where Bruce broke down in sobs. Excavation of the site began the next day. The victims were found fully clothed in a crouching position. Reggie had somehow broken his tape and was holding Carol's hand. There was two feet of dirt over their heads. With ten years of homicide under his belt, Detective Meacham said it was one of the saddest and most horrible things he had ever seen. The medical examiner determined that both Reggie and Carol were alive in the hole before they were buried. Their nostrils, mouths, throats, esophagi, and trachea had fine sprays of dirt in them, which indicated that they had inhaled it. They died from mechanical asphyxiation and smothering, caused by the dirt covering their heads while compressing their chests. She said it was the worst case of asphyxiation she'd ever seen. It was "horrendous."

At some point while in jail, but unaware that Bruce had come clean, Michael's grandmother called him.

Grandma: Michael, listen to me and don't say a word. You're in the newspaper. All over the newspaper yesterday and today

Michael: For what?

Grandma: Murder

Michael: What?!

Grandma: Murder. 'Bodies ID'd as former South Carolina couple James and Carol Sumner. Bail was denied for 18-year-old Bruce Nixon of Florida who was arrested and charged with murder, home invasion, robbery, and kidnapping.' He took them to the grave site and everything

Michael: Oh my God. Are you kidding me?

Grandma: It's right here in today's paper

Michael: Bruce took them to the f*****g spot. The f****r showed them where the spot was at?

Grandma: Yes, dear

Michael: *starts panting* Bruce just killed us all

Bruce Nixon told detectives everything that had happened and agreed to testify on behalf of the prosecution. He wasn't sentenced until after he testified against the other three group members, but in the end, he received 45 years for each victim, currently being served concurrently at Century Correctional Institution in Florida. Alan Wade was tried first.

Michael Jackson was the first to be tried. Testifying on his own behalf, Michael stated that the plan was only to rob the Sumners and that it was not going to involve murder. He said that Alan and Bruce went into the house and when they came out they drove off in the Lincoln which he then followed. He claims he had no idea that Reggie and Carol were in the trunk. According to Michael, when they arrived at the hole in Georgia, it was Alan and Bruce who told him where to park and to bring them a flashlight. It was when he arrived at the burial site that he heard Carol moan. He then stated that he questioned what the other two were doing before returning to the Mazda to wait. He did admit to impersonating Reggie. Bruce testified that Michael had been the ringleader and was the one who orchestrated everything. After stepping down from the witness stand, Carol's daughter, Rhonda, said of Bruce, "I just wanted to hug him. He is a murderer, but in the end, he did the right thing." It was that testimony that she believed sealed Michael's fate because he was found guilty of first degree murder, robbery, and kid-napping, and sentenced to death for each murder. He is currently on death row in Florida.

Alan was next to be tried. Two witnesses who were not identified gave victim impact statements during the penalty phase. Alan's lawyer then called six of their own witnesses to testify including Bruce Nixon,

Alan's mom and sister, the mother of a friend, his middle school principal, and his youth pastor. Overall, the witnesses testified that Alan's parents divorced when he was eight and his father disappeared from his life. His mother took him to church regularly and as a kid, he was kind, smart, and well-behaved. After the divorce, his mother was unable to spend a lot of time with him because she had to work a lot to support them. When he was in his teens, his mother had a bout with breast cancer. By his early teens, he began to use drugs. In the sixth grade, he was involuntarily committed to a 72-hour hold because of a drug related incident. When he was sixteen, his mom had to take him out of school or be arrested for his truancy. The next year, his mother kicked him out of the house in an attempt at tough love because his drug use was becoming worse. In 2004 Alan introduced her to Michael, whom she immediately saw as a bad influence on him. Since his arrest and before his trial, Alan had apparently become a model prisoner, obtained his G.E.D and tutored other inmates in math. Nothing seemed to sway the jury, however, because he was found guilty on all counts and voted eleven-to-one to receive the death penalty. He is also currently on death row in Florida.

Tiffany was the last to be tried. Her lawyer argued that she wasn't a major participant in the crimes. He said that she was under the control of her boyfriend Michael, and that he was the mastermind. Tiffany claimed that she believed the crime would only constitute a simple theft and that she didn't knowingly participate in the robberies, kidnapping or murders. She insisted that she did not know that Reggie and Carol were in the trunk of the Lincoln until they arrived at the burial site. The circuit judge, Michael Weatherby did not see it that way, stating that it was she who held the flashlight during the digging of the grave and was there when they were bound and placed in the trunk. He also noted that she was the one who purchased the duct tape and gloves and later pawned the jewelry and computer they had stolen. "She was thoroughly involved," Weatherby stated. "She knew exactly what she was doing and participated without hesitation." It was noted as well that she was the only one of the four who had previously known the Sumners. During the penalty phase, the prosecution called two of the victim's family members who gave impact statements. The defense attorney then called up witnesses who testified that Tiffany was of good character. Three of those witnesses were correctional officers who stated that Tiffany had been no trouble in jail and did not cause any problems. A psychiatrist, Dr. Earnest Miller, testified that she suffered from poly-substance and alcohol abuse, chronic depression, and a personality disorder. He also stated that she had witnessed abuse to family members and had been sexually abused herself by her stepfather. On the other hand, he testified that Tiffany was competent and thus he could not support a plea of insanity. Finally, he stated that she knew right from wrong and had a high average IQ. In the end, Tiffany was also found guilty of all charges and sentenced to death by a 9-3 vote. Upon hearing her fate, she bowed her head and turned to her mother, mouthing the words "I love you". Her lawyer, Quentin Till, said she had been ready for the decision. He visited her in jail that week. "I told her to be strong," he said. "...I still see her being utilized and manipulated by Michael Jackson." Revis Sumner, Reggie's brother, said that Tiffany has since written to the family, asking for forgiveness. He says he has forgiven her, but that doesn't mean she shouldn't suffer for her actions. The Reverend Jean Clark, Reggie's sister has said, "I pray for Tiffany. I pray for all of them. I'm grieved that these four young people have wasted their lives." Chief Assistant State Attorney, Jay Plotkin, who tried all four cases said, "All of these defendants got exactly what they deserved. Justice was done." After the sentences were given and the trials were over, Reggie's son, Frederick Hallock, said, "You expect some sort of closure or some sort of good feeling when the verdict is read, but it didn't seem to help much. I just know they didn't deserve this." Currently, Tiffany is one of only five women on Florida's death row. At the time of her sentence, she was the sole woman there.

Tiffany, Michael, and Alan all filed appeals after their trials, citing multiple issues. All three were denied and their sentences were upheld. Recently, in 2015, Tiffany filed another appeal, asking for a new trial. She claims that her defense lawyers were ineffective and that she should not have been convicted of first-degree murder since she did not actually bury the bodies herself. But according to Florida law, it doesn't matter who actually committed the murder. Just knowing that it was going to happen is enough to warrant a guilty verdict. At her original trial Tiffany said, "But please remember I didn't do this. I am not the monster that created this, but I regret meeting him," referring to Michael. Upon hearing that Tiffany was asking for a new trial, Reggie's sister, Jean had this to say: "Most people are going to try to come back with something like that after the fact, because they're going to try to find a loophole and get off. But justice has a voice, and justice has to be served." And the thought of going through another trial breaks her heart. "I have family members that are still not the same and never will be the same. In fact, I don't like to involve them too much into things like this, because they can't deal with it."

In 2014, Alan Wade also filed an appeal for a new trial, citing that his lawyers did not do a good job of representing him. His appellate lawyers said that his original defense lawyers barely met with him before the trial and didn't interview witnesses prior to putting them on the stand. They also cited the lack of objections to supposedly questionable evidence. In December 2014, it was decided by the Supreme Court of Florida that his conviction be upheld.

Previous to that, Michael Jackson filed an appeal for a new trial, stating that his lawyers were also ineffective. As with Alan's trial, Michael claims that his lawyers did not make objections to certain evidence when there was clearly an objection to be made. The judge did allow an appeal hearing for his concerns and at the close of the hearing, Michael was allowed to make a statement. It went as follows:

First, I'd like to say that I am guilty of the crimes of first-degree murder, kidnapping, and robbery against Mr. and Mrs. Sumner. My reason for wanting to address the Court today is because of the many lies I told to everyone years ago at pretrial and then trial. I downplayed my involvement to look as if I were not guilty but the truth is that—the truth is that it was my idea to do this. Truly, I did not make anyone do anything. All were willing participants but I was, in fact, the leader. It was my idea to do it. I lied to this Court all throughout my trial testimony, same to [defense counsel and the State]. Even more so I lied to the people who deserve the truth the most, the family of Mr. and Mrs. Sumner, and for that, I am deeply sorry. There are no words that I could ever offer that would convey the depth of my remorse or sorrow, but again I say that I am truly sorry for what I have done and though I'm undeserving, I do ask forgiveness. My desire today is to reconcile the truth to the family of Mr. and Mrs. Sumner and to Your Honor, the attorneys and to the Court record. If necessary, I will answer any and all questions fully and truthfully. Thank you.

His conviction was upheld. Tiffany, Michael, Alan, and Bruce remain in jail today, with the former three on death row.

"It's sad," said Rhonda Alford about her parents. "It took them so long to find each other." Carol and Reggie's ashes sit in an urn in Rhonda's home, forever mixed and blended together.

DRUG CRAZED KILLER : THE TRUE STORY OF ROSIE ALFARO

91

ELIZABETH MARKS

Maria del Rosio Alfaro, better known to the media a Rosie Alfaro, is the first woman to be sentenced to death in Orange County. Her story is a tragic one, set in a town nearby Disneyland in Anaheim, California. By the time that Rosie was thirteen, she was heavily into drugs and considered by many to be an addict. At this age, Rosie was often doing fifty speedballs a day for weeks at a time, a speedball being a mixture of heroin and cocaine. Regular doses of this highly addictive cocktail were just the first steps along a dark path, and in grade seven she dropped out of school. By the time that Rosie was fourteen years old, she had become a prostitute. Despite efforts from her mother to get her back on track, a tormented and abused past pushed her forward on her path of self-destruction

At the witness stand in a court case only a few years after this point in her life, an old friend of Rosie's Tamara Benedict testified that at that time they both often slept with drug dealers for money so that they could buy drugs. Sometimes just receive their payment in narcotics directly. Benedict claimed "we had no jobs at all" and "sometimes we would steal from stores or get someone to steal for us." By the time that Rosie was fifteen, she was a single mother. At 18, she was a mother of two and pregnant with twins. It is also at this age that she committed the murder that would ruin her life.

When Rosie had been pregnant with her second child, she had spent some time living at the Wallace residence, the family of one of her friends from school. The Wallace's had three girls, Amber, April, and Autumn. Rosie was friends with April Wallace and was taking shelter at their house during one of the most difficult periods of her life. After her time living with the family, she got back into drugs, became distant, and had very little contact. The only time that she would have any association with the family would be when she was offered a lift somewhere.

A year later, when Rosie had had the baby and was pregnant with the twins, she was living with a relative of the father from her most recent pregnancy. This house was three blocks away from the Wallace residence. Rosie was on another drug binge at the time and had her first hit at eleven in the morning. By 2 PM she was getting desperate for another fix. She began to think about how she could acquire the money for more drugs. She mentioned to the men that she was with, the three of them looking after her oldest child, that she had an old video camera that she had left at the Wallace residence. She asked them to drive her to the residence so that she could retrieve it, and that she would gladly trade this camera in for cash so that they could all get another hit. The two men, Rosie, and her eldest boy who was only fourteen months old at the time drove to the Wallace residence. Rosie got out by herself to go and knock at the door, and the two men stood outside of the car with the baby. Rosie has made different testimonies in her time, both claiming that she didn't know that nine-year-old Autumn Wallace would be home and that she did realize. Whichever of these is true, Rosie knocked on the front door and

Autumn answered. Based on her testimonies, it is more likely that she was expecting Autumn to be home so that somebody would enable her to get inside of the house.

Autumn's school had had an 'early day' that afternoon, and they had let the children leave at 2:35PM. Her mother wasn't due home from work until after five, and neither of her sisters were home. Rosie asked if she would be able to use their bathroom to fix her hair and freshen herself up. Autumn, who remembered Rosie from the time that she spent living with the family, didn't hesitate to let her in. Before Rosie had knocked at the door, Autumn had been cutting out paper dolls. She went back to her task in the living room. On her way to the bathroom, Rosie went to the kitchen and picked up a knife. In the bathroom, she created a ruse to trick Autumn. She claimed that she needed assistance with an eyelash curler, and asked Autumn to come into the bathroom to help her. When Autumn entered the bathroom, Rosie grabbed her. "That's when I did it," Alfaro told the investigators. "I stabbed her . . . 'cause she knew who I was," Rosie claims that Autumn made no sound when she was attacked and that nobody else was involved. "I was too high; I just remember her looking at me," Alfaro when she was interviewed at Orange County Jail. "Before, sometimes at night, the day would come back, and I'd block that out. Now I think about it more and more, because blocking is not working." Alfaro attacked Autumn with such ferocity that she died on the spot.

In all of Rosie's later testimonies, she claims that she was forced to stab the girl by one of the men who had accompanied her. She also claims that she stabbed Autumn several times, but that she did not finish the deed. Whether Rosie acted alone or with this man who she still refuses to identify, Autumn Wallace was stabbed fifty-seven times in her face, chest, and back. After this time, Rosie claims that she and the man went around the house stealing a few items. They took a portable TV, a typewriter, a telephone and a Nintendo set. Later on, they sold these items for a mere $300. As Rosie began to come down off her high, she realized the severity of the things that she had done and the guilt began to set in. She began to panic, and it was then that she made plans for her escape.

At 5:15 PM, April Wallace returned home. She found the door unlocked and the house in a mess. She called out to Autumn but got no response. She immediately ran to the house across the street for safety where she could wait for her mother to come home. Linda Wallace, the girls' mother, arrived home at 5:40 PM. She was told that her house had been burgled and that Autumn was missing. Believing that her girl might be hiding, she went inside the house to search for the youngest daughter and found her in the back bathroom in a pool of blood. Neighbors told Linda that they had seen a brownish Monte Carlo parked outside of the Wallace house and that two men were standing outside of the car. One of them was holding a small child. Police fingerprinted the house and found prints that matched

Alfaro's. They brought Rosie in for questioning, and she denied any involvement in the murder, or that she has been near the house at all. As they didn't have any further evidence or a witness that could identify her having been at the house, Rosie was let go.

At some point after the murder, Rosie asked one of her friends if she could leave a bag full of clothing outside of their house. She had made plans to leave for Mexico the next day, and wanted this bag to be easily accessible. However, Rosie never showed up. Investigators found out about the bag and inside they found a pair of Alfaro's tennis shoes and a pair of April Wallace's boots stolen from the house. They put out a warrant of arrest for Alfaro, and brought her in for questioning again. It was at this point that Alfaro began to realize that she wouldn't get away with the crime, and that she would have to be more cooperative with the police.

Alfaro identified one of the men that she had been with as Antonio Reynoso, being the man who stayed in the car with her son. Antonio had been released from prison the previous day. He had agreed to share his drugs with Rosie is she was happy to share her needle. The other man, who Rosie claims was active in the killing of Autumn Wallace, she has persistently refused to identify over the years, and only refers to by the name of Beto. Alfaro has said several times in court that she is not able to identify this man for the police as she fears for the safety of her children and her partner. Even if the face of the death penalty, Rosie did not reveal the identity of this man, and he still remains a mystery. Some members of the court have claimed that they feel the story of Beto is a fabrication, and that Rosie committed the crime by herself. However, there is some evidence to suggest that her claims might be true. Not only did neighbors see the two men out the front of the house, but a footprint in the bathroom that was initially thought to belong to Rosie was found to not match the shoes that she had been wearing. While all of the prints had initially been assumed to be Alfaro's, criminologist Marc Taylor found that there was also another set of prints both inside and outside of the house. This gives some credibility to Alfaro's story, but her unwillingness to identify the man means that she is taking the full consequences for the situation alone. Alfaro claims that when Beto saw that Autumn was home, he became enraged and put a knife to Rosie's back. He threatened to stab her if she wasn't going to stab Autumn. Rosie admits to stabbing Autumn several times, but maintains that Beto was the one who did the majority of the stabbing and caused Autumn's death. "If I wasn't so scared my family would get hurt, I'd tell the truth, but I just can't," she said in court. Even though it means that she is potentially getting the death sentence for a crime that she didn't solely commit, she remains silent on this issue in order to protect her family.

As Rosie plans to die with the identity of Beto, it is likely that this person will never be brought to justice and remains at large. Rosie initially claimed that the man was a friend of her father's, and that his name was Miguel. Later she claimed that this was not true and that the man who she would only name as Beto had a woman's name tattooed on the side of his neck. Alfaro identified a photo of the man. Orange County investigator Robert Harper identified the likely identity of this man to be Robert Frias Gonzalez, but Rosie gave no confirmation of this suspicion. It was later revealed the that tattoo on the side of his man's neck was actually a butterfly, but due to Rosie's state of mind and drug abuse her claims have not been judged as entirely false. It is impossible to say whether Rosie was identifying a photograph just to appease the police, and that this explains the difference between the tattoos, whether she was in such a state of mind that she couldn't remember the tattoo correctly, or whether the man had any identifiable tattoos done over with larger and darker designs to hide what was underneath. The fact that there is a discrepancy between the tattoos certainly doesn't factor this final consideration. Perhaps if his tattoo was the name is a lost loved one, he marked it with a butterfly to keep his display of respect? A deputy sheriff at the Orange County jail testified that he had seen a man similar to the one that Rosie had identified in the picture getting into a blue Camaro outside of the Orange County jail. From the evidence, it would certainly seem that another person was present at the residence and may have had involvement in the murder of Autumn Wallace, but without Alfaro's testimony on this matter nothing more can be pursued.

In the courtroom Alfaro, wearing a floral blouse and blue stretch pants, cried throughout Tamara Benedict's testimony and also those of her childhood friends, her boyfriend

Manuel Cueva, and her mother Silvia Melendez Alfaro. When Cueva described the visits of Alfaro's children to the County jail as Rosie awaited trial, she openly sobbed. Sylvia Alfaro made every attempt possible to try to create some sympathy and understanding for Rosie, painting an image of the horrific childhood that she had suffered through. Sylvia testified that her husband was a dreadful alcoholic who regularly hit her and Rosie in front of the other children in the family. He would also often throw the whole family out of the house when he was in a drunken rage. Alfaro's mother discussed Rosie's early drug use and how she seemed totally unable to quit her habits, constantly seeking to get some distance from the real world. When Rosie was pregnant with her first child at the age of fourteen, her father left home and abandoned the family. Sylvia claimed that Rosie completely lost control of her drug addiction at the age of fifteen. "She wore heavy makeup, black clothes and was always dirty. She didn't care how she looked." From this point until when Rosie attacked Autumn, she was in an almost constant state of pregnancy. With no other way to support her habit, she slept with her dealers and attempted to look after her children as best she could.

A mental health expert, Dr. Consuelo Edwards, was the first one that Rosie had told about Beto. It was Edwards that recommended that she should speak about Beto in court, and he also came forward to defend her with his testimony. From his interactions with Rosie, Edwards deemed that her intellectual functioning was 'borderline' and that he feels that she has a serious learning disability. He didn't argue that he felt this excused any of her behavior, but that it should be something to factor when the jury are arriving at their decision. He tested Rosie as having an IQ of 78, and testified that her intellectual issues were made worse by the traumatic experiences that she had gone through as a child. In reaction to these claims, the prosecutor called forth several employees at the Orange County jail who testified to Rosie's poor behavior in jail. These employees also claimed that they had heard Rosie saying "I'm a frustrated person who takes things out on people, and have to learn to live with that," and "I'm not going to be able to do this again. I'm no actor. I'm going to be cold this time. I just want to get this over with." It is not certain whether this was a move to try to paint Rosie as an inherently bad or disturbed person, as this claims as nothing to do with her capacity intellectually. Perhaps they were making the argument that Rosie's lack of intellectual giftedness mean that she wasn't able to reflect on her own behavior and that way that she treated others. However these testimonies were intended, they painted Rosie as incredibly difficult to deal with and as somebody who lashes out with quick and ill-thought-through responses.

The first jury that assessed the case was on 14th July 1992. The judge for this case claimed that her crime was the most "senseless, brutal, vicious, and callous killing" that he had ever known. The jury was a deadlock with 10:2 in favor of Rosie receiving the death penalty, meaning that this was not enough to hand down the sentence. A deadlock means that the required amounts of votes was not reached, and in order to place a person on Death Row every member of the jury needed to agree that this was the proper course of action according to the evidence that they had viewed during the case. When Rosie was reflecting on this outcome and how close she had come to being sentenced to death, she claimed that "I do think that someone has to pay for what happened to that poor little girl, and that's me," she said. "But I can't help thinking how my life stopped, ended, at 18, and that I have no future, and all that is because of drugs." In many ways, Alfaro has distanced herself not only from the person that she was when she committed the crime, but the person who engaged in the type of lifestyle that she did before that. As she awaited her next trial date, she claimed that she would spend all day trying not to think about how likely it was that she would be sentenced to death and instead thought about the ways in which drugs had wasted her life.

Then in 2007, another court hearing was held where the jury placed forward the unanimous decision for the death sentence. During this trial, Rosie claimed that she was constantly haunted by her actions. She read out a letter that she had written to Autumn. "I have a picture of you in my Bible, and every time I open it, I see your innocent face and I think of my boys and what I would do if something were ever to happen to them. . . . So please know that I am deeply and truly sorry, Autumn, and I will pay for the rest of my life for what happened." Nobody can be sure whether this was an attempt to show remorse and soften the approach of the jury or whether Alfaro simply felt the need to be able to express these feelings in a more public context than she was capable of in jail. Perhaps Alfaro wanted for the Wallace family to hear that she was experiencing remorse over the issue, and that she was making a genuine attempt to comprehend and suffer for the things that she had done. When the sentence was handed down, Deputy Dist. Atty. Charles J. Middleton described the jury's decision as "justified" and claims that he knew the outcome based on the amount of time that the jury took considering the evidence, saying "I was sure it was a death verdict because I could not imagine 12 people agreeing that soon that this kind of a crime should not get a death sentence." These jury members deliberated for just over two days before they released their unanimous recommendation. When the sentence was handed down, it was met with clapping and cheering from the Wallace family and gasps and shock from the Alfaros and their supporters. Alfaro later claimed: "I know it's hard for the Wallaces to forgive me, and I don't ask for their forgiveness," Alfaro said. "If it had been one of my kids that was killed—I'm a mother too—I'd probably do the same thing: celebrate." William M. Monroe, who was Alfaro's attorney, quoted Alfaro as saying "I can't believe this. It can't happen to me. . . . Why did they (jurors) do this?" after the sentence was brought down. Monroe also made some emotional claims, seemingly unable to believe that Alfaro was truly going to be placed on Death Row. "I'm probably as shocked by the verdict as Rosie Alfaro is," Monroe said outside the courtroom. "I still contend that this crime was committed by a person with an abandoned and malignant heart, and Rosie Alfaro is not (such) a person." Monroe mentioned that "I feel terrible, absolutely terrible for what happened to Autumn Wallace, but this little girl, this young woman-child, does not deserve" and that he would file an appeal. After the verdict was served, photographers and cameramen were crowded around the courthouse hoping to catch a glimpse of the grief-ridden Alfaro. Alfaro supporters shielded their faces and turned their backs in an attempt to avoid the media. "Nobody wants to talk right now. We have no words," said a friend of the defendant. As with all cases, there was a lot of initial hype but it slowly died down. Now, when searching about the Alfaro case, there is rarely a recent article that will give any updates or further information on the matter. Rosie is simply on Death Row awaiting her visit to the gas chamber as her sons continue to grow up without her presence.

Much of the coverage around the case has regarded the behavior and quotes of the two mothers in the courtroom: Linda Wallace the mother of the deceased Autumn who claimed to fight for justice for her daughter's death, and Sylvia Alfaro who was fighting for the life of her own daughter. Linda Wallace made an emotional plea to the courtroom, claiming that during the trial her daughter has only been known as a young victim stabbed to death by somebody that she trusted. The grieving mother wanted everybody to know what Autumn was really like, and that was she so much more than the court case had reduced her to. She spoke about her blonde hair and brown eyes, and that she was an A student who loved swimming and fishing. She was incredibly creative, and wanted to be an artist when she grew up. Of Rosie, Linda claimed that what she did is horrible and that she will "never forgive or forget her." To Sylvia Alfaro, Linda said that she really felt for her because she knows what it feels like to lose a daughter.

Sylvia Alfaro was similarly trying to expand the way that the people in court were viewing her daughter, saying that "The first time that I came here, I felt like I was sitting in the electric chair," she cried. "I beg you, please forgive my daughter and please forgive what she did," Sylvia claimed that Rosie's issues with drugs had gotten a lot worse after the birth of her daughter's first son Daniel, and that she had enrolled her daughter in several drug programs in an attempt to beat her habits. Unfortunately, she always went back to her old ways after a few months. However, Sylvia maintains that while Rosie was pregnant she usually managed to control her drug addiction. This does not align with the information that was presented before the court on the day of Autumn Wallace's murder. This particular binge might well have been an isolated event or even an extended period of drug usage, but in either case, it would have been difficult for the jury to believe that Rosie was not a drug user during pregnancies when the entire case revolved around her desperation for another hit. Sylia had even gone so far as to sent her daughter to Mexico to live with her grandmother in the hope that this distance and change of environment would help her to get away from the complicated lifestyle around drugs, but this change in location didn't make any difference. She ended up coming back home when her grandmother was not able to cope with her behavior, and she fell into the same patterns.

Monroe, the attorney, attempted to raise some sympathy for Rosie regarding her troubled past and attempted to make the case that she should be sent to prison instead of the gas chamber. He made this assertion based on her addiction to drugs and her being the mother of four young boys. He claimed that the jury made a mistake in their recommendation, and he also introduced the notion of race. Monroe claimed that the mainly white jury could not possibly understand what it was to grow up in a household like Rosie had, and that they could not "empathize, understand or relate" to Latino women trapped in the drug world. While it might be true that somebody in a very different demographic cannot fully understand the life of somebody who has endured so much pain, the purpose of a jury is to find a random sampling of people who can determine what they feel is just action and what behavior should be acceptable in our society. Regardless of Alfaro's abuse in her childhood and early teens, the murder of a nine-year-old girl is not something that the jury considered as acceptable behavior.

Linda Wallace and her daughters had been traveling from their new homes in Lake Havasu , Arizona, the girls both having married and started their own families. April Nunez and Amber Szabo had been traveling in support of their deceased sister and trying to come to terms with her loss. In one interview, their mother Linda claimed that "You would think after all this time, you would get over it, but you don't." When asked how she endured through a trial, two penalty hearings, and a fifteen-year wait for the appellate review, Linda claimed that "I was doing it for Autumn." Later she also claimed that "it's the only thing I can do for her," the mom said, "I need to be there to represent her because she can't do it. I go to be with my daughter." Linda Wallace has also confided in several interviews how she feels outside of the court. "The hardest thing for me is to see people now who are Autumn's age," she said. "Not being able to see her grow up, that's what bothers me the most. She would be 26 years old now. She could be married. She could have kids. That's what I think about." Linda says that she has spent the years waiting for justice, and not spending her time or energy thinking about Alfaro. "I know she is in a bad place," Wallace says. "I know she will never see the light of day. I am fine with it." Linda also commented that Alfaro hasn't had much of a life since her arrest: "she just exists," the mother said. "It wouldn't be any life I would want." While the Wallace mother was one of the members of the family who was clapping when the sentence was passed down and has also been somebody to proclaim often and loudly that her daughter needs justice, she has also stated that she doesn't feel the need for Alfaro to be executed. In some ways, this might be an attempt to show a soft side to the media as in many of her interviews she claims that she waited fifteen years for the sentence to be handed down, when Alfaro had been imprisoned for that entire duration. This suggests that, in some way, Linda Wallace did feel that it was necessary for Rosie to be put on Death Row to properly avenge Autumn's death.

April and Amber have expressed similar long-lasting hatred of Rosie. "We get nothing," Zabo said. "And she gets all of these things. It makes me mad. ... I just want to see her be put to death, and I want to see it faster than it is taking." When April was asked if she would travel to San Quentin Prison to watch Alfaro get executed, she said "Oh yes, I would go to watch her die, without a doubt. I would do it myself if they'd let me." Linda Wallace was also asked in the same interview, she responded "I am not that much for that," she said. "If she is put to death, then another mother loses her child. I know what it feels like to lose a child." But her other interactions with the media suggest that Rosie getting the death penalty gave her some sense of relief and faith in the system.

The judge, Middleton, claimed that Monroe did not give any credence to Monroe's claims of racial misconception, and asserted that the jury had made their decision purely based on facts. He went on to say that she made her own choices in life and that Rosie cannot blame her action on others no matter how poor her treatment as a child and young adult had been. He also put forward the opinion that based on the evidence in court he did not believe that Rosie Alfaro was capable of looking after her children. Alfaro was convicted of first-degree murder with special circumstances, the circumstances being that the murder offered during the felonies of Burglary and Robbery. Alfaro joined two other women on Death Row, Maureen McDermott and Cynthia Lynn Coffman. McDermott was a Los Angeles registered nurse who was convicted in 1990 of hiring a co-worker to murder her roommate. It was found that Maureen planned to collect on a $100 00 mortgage insurance policy. Coffman was convicted in 1986 of the kidnapping and murder of a woman in San Bernardino. Capital punishment was restored in California in 1978, and these are the only three women to receive the death penalty in that time.

Since she was handed down the death sentence, Alfaro says that she spends her time thinking about how misguided her drug addled youth was, what happened to Autumn, and the days when her children will be old enough to know what she did. "God, I hate to think of the future, because there's not a future for me and my kids," she said. "It's going to be up to (them) if they still want to call me mom when they find out. I know they're going to find out sooner or later, and I'm scared of what they're going to decide." Alfaro is now 44 years old and still on Death Row with his four children still being cared for by boyfriend Cueva. She will not get to see them grow up, and may not feel that she deserves to give them any guidance in doing so. In many ways, she is now waiting for death as she no longer has a functional life. Waiting for the nightmare to be over do that she no longer has to block out the deeds of her past.

JASMINE RICHARDSON

GERTRUDE SCOTT

On the South Saskatchewan River in Alberta, Canada is a town called Medicine Hat. With a population of just over 60,000 it is filled with little communities where everybody knows everybody. With a relatively low crime rate and virtually none of those crimes involving homicide it's the perfect place to raise a family in a safe environment, or at least it would seem that way I should I say. The security offered by Medicine Hat was greatly diminished when the entire town was shaken to its core in April of 2006.

On April 23, 2006 the community was rocked to its very foundation with the discovery of a gruesome triple homicide. An entire family was found stabbed to death in their home that day. The bodies were discovered by the 8 year old boy's best friend when he arrived at the house to get his friend to come out and play. When cops were notified and an investigation began the scene revealed was one of the worst scenes in Canadian history. Debra Richardson, 48 and her husband Marc, 42 were found in the basement with multiple stab wounds covering their bodies and upon further investigation their son 8 year old Jacob was found also stabbed to death with his throat slit in his bed upstairs. Such a horrific scene was left behind that the police responding would be affected long after the investigation. It didn't take police long to realize that family photos around the home depicted a family of 4 instead of 3. The 12 year old daughter Jasmine was missing. Immediately police were concerned that they had a kidnapping on their hands. The sweet angelic looking daughter in the photos must have been victimized by the monster that did this to her family as well. However, the sweet loving family photos that the police encountered depicting a 12 year old girl were not the reality where Jasmine was concerned. Jasmine had started acting and dressing differently. She had new friends, she was getting in trouble and going off to wild parties and she had a 23 year old boyfriend that her parents detested here being with. That boyfriend was into drugs, drinking, and dark things like werewolves, vampires, and the Goth culture. In fact that boyfriend even claimed to be a werewolf himself and reportedly professed to liking the taste of blood. Jasmine Richardson was not missing because she had been kidnapped rather she was missing because she was responsible. It would be later discovered that Jasmine and her 23 year old boyfriend, Jeremy Steinke had committed the murders themselves and had gone on the run.

Background

Once upon a time Jasmine Richardson was the sweet little girl depicted in the family photos around the Richardson house. Once upon a time the family was the perfect poster family for suburban bliss but something went wrong. Jasmine became interested in the Goth culture as well as the Wiccan religion. With this interest came a dark side to the little girl.

At 12 the little girl looked much older; perhaps 15 or 16 and she even claimed to be that old on social media. Soon she had the attention of local man Jeremy Steinke. Jasmine and Jeremy fell into a dangerous relationship. They idolized a life of negativity. They dressed in dark fantasy type clothing and they frequented sites on the internet like vampire freaks, a social media site for teens that love all things vampire. In fact Jeremy himself claimed to love the taste of blood and that he was a 300 year old werewolf. Jeremy had more practice at the twisted lifestyle that they both began to lead than Jasmine did but he was also weakened by a controlling effect that Jasmine had on him. Jasmine knew how to manipulate Jeremy. In many ways this seemed to spell love for Jeremy; he had found a girl that he would do anything for. In Jasmine's case Jeremy was an adult that she could control. She might have to live under what felt like the tyranny of her parents and she might have to go by the rules at the strict Catholic school that she attended but with Jeremy she had the say so. She could only wish for something and Jeremy was there to try to make her wishes come true. This might all sound like the musings of a warped but innocent mind, a reality created by dissatisfied kids looking to feel like they have more control over their lives but Jasmine and Jeremy took things much farther than most kids would dare to go. Just like any good loving parents the Richardsons became alarmed when they learned of the changes in their daughter's lifestyle. The most alarming thing to Jasmine's parents was Jeremy. No parent is going to be comfortable with their 12 year old little girl being in a relationship with a 23 year old man. More alarmingly their relationship was sexual as well. Jasmine may have looked much older but she still had the mind and body of a 12 year old girl chronologically speaking.

When Jasmine told Jeremy online that she had a plan to kill her family he hopped on board. They wrote instant messages to each other discussing the killing of Jasmine's family. Below are the exact words they typed to each other in a snippet of their conversation.

Jasmine: "I have this plan. It begins with me killing them and ends with me living with you."

Jeremy: "I love your plan but we need to get a little more creative with like details and stuff."

Who knows now if either of them were truly serious about committing the murders in the beginning but in the end Jeremy got pumped up watching the movie *Natural Born Killers,* got drunk, did some lines of cocaine and then he was ready to help his beloved carry out her request to alleviate herself of her bothersome parents. All it took was a set of loving protective parents trying to protect their 12 year old daughter from the psychological and perhaps even physical damage that would come from having a sexual relationship with a 23 year old man and Jasmine and Jeremy were all too ready to put an end to the two nuisances trying to keep them apart.

On the night of April 22nd Jeremy watched *Natural Born Killers* with his friends, did some drinking and drugs and then he was ready. He would do anything to make Jasmine happy. Despite her young age and the considerable age gap between the two Jasmine knew how to manipulate Jeremy. Jeremy snuck into the basement of The

Richardson's split level home and waited. Thinking she heard noises Debra Richardson, already in her night gown, went down to investigate. She couldn't have been prepared for what awaited her. As soon as Debra flipped on the light switch Jeremy attacked her stabbing her 12 times before killing her. Debra's husband Marc was close behind after hearing the commotion and armed with a screwdriver. However, in the end his screwdriver was no match for Jeremy's knife. Later Jeremy would tell an undercover police officer that he was worried Marc would get the better of him and that Marc nearly succeeded in defending himself with that screwdriver. No matter the fight Marc put up the scene ended up with him on the floor still in a defensive stance, dead with 24 stab wounds. Later Jeremy would say that Marc asked 'why' just before he died and Jeremy replied, 'it's what your daughter wanted.'

After killing Marc and Debra Jeremy headed upstairs leaving a trail of blood in his wake. Upstairs Jasmine was trying to calm her little brother down. At this point Jeremy and Jasmine's stories are not the same. Both of them say it was the other that actually killed the little boy. I suppose we will never know the truth nevertheless young Jacob was found in his bed with stab wounds in his body and his throat slit side to side. Jasmine and Jeremy left the scene and reportedly went back to a friend's apartment to have sex after obliterating Jasmine's entire family. They were the outlaw lovers that they had dreamed of being bound together even more so by the horrific blood bath they had just caused. The two went on the run but they didn't make it far. After a search of Jasmine's school locker a graphic picture surfaced of a girl's whole family burning in a fire while she laughs and escapes with her boyfriend. When police saw this drawing they went from searching for Jasmine as a victim to searching for her as a suspect.

Jasmine and Jeremy were apprehended in Saskatchewan the very next day after the bodies of her family were discovered. The pair were reportedly laughing and joking around with friends about the murders only one day after they had taken place.

Unfathomable Murder

The Richardsons were the picturesque family living in a picturesque neighborhood. Ross Glen, the community where the Richardsons lived, was a middle class neighborhood full of working class families. Their neighbors on one side were Sara and her six year old son Gareth, Jacob's best friend, and their neighbors on the other side were Phyllis and Vernon Gehring. The Gehrings were an elderly couple that liked to garden and look after their dog, a shi tzu Bishon mix. Often the scene would be that Gareth and Jacob could be found playing in the backyard as children do and the Gehrings would delight in tossing balls back over the fence when they strayed a bit too far. The Gehrings felt like Jacob kept them young. They admittedly didn't know much about the daughter. Just the night before that fateful afternoon when the bodies were found Marc Richardson had grilled hot dogs in the backyard for the boys while the Gehring's dog played with the Richardson family's dog through the fence. Everything seemed perfect in that sleepy little neighborhood until that fateful afternoon on April 23rd when Gareth went looking for his best friend.

It was about 1pm and Sara and Gareth had been at Sara's mom's house but Gareth had been asking to play with Jacob all morning. When Gareth could not get anyone to answer the phone at the Richardson residence Sara told him that they could go to the movies. Gareth was still bummed out about not getting to see Jacob and when he and his mom returned home before heading to the movies he darted over to the Richardson's after seeing that Marc's white pickup truck was in the driveway. Gareth knocked on the door but there was no answer, as a curious little boy might he began peering into the basement windows of the split level home. When he saw lifeless bodies and a basement covered in blood he ran back to his mom to tell her what he'd seen. Although Gareth wasn't usually the type of boy to make up stories the things he was saying to Sara just didn't make sense. As she followed him over to the neighbor's house she warned him that he had better not be lying. Sadly Gareth was not lying. When she peered through the same windows that Gareth had Sara saw a horrible scene in front of her. She was afraid that the intruder that had done this was still around, maybe he was even in her house waiting for her and Gareth. She called her mom and her mom told her she had to call 911. Sara's mom and the police headed to the scene. What would unfold at that crime scene would haunt police officers that investigated for years to come. Some of the officers involved were touched so much by young Jacob's defiled body that they broke down on the stand months later when they had to talk about it.

The police came in thinking that they might have an intruder still lurking about the property. They entered with caution. What they saw was unfathomable. There were the bodies of a man and woman in the basement both covered in blood. The woman, Debra Richardson was slumped in the floor with her night gown hiked up exposing the fact that all she had been wearing when she was attacked was that night gown. There was blood all over her and a pool of blood all around her. The little black family dog was standing beside her. Perhaps he felt that he needed to protect her but sadly it was too late for that. Across the basement slumped against a wall was Marc Richardson. His hands were straight out as though he were trying to defend himself. He was frozen by rigor mortis in a defensive state that did nothing for his defense in the end. Marc was wearing only black boxer shorts and a screwdriver was lying beside him. He, too, was riddled with stab wounds. The entire basement was covered in splatters of blood, there had been a real struggle between the Richardsons and their assailant. Upon further investigation of the house the police came across their worst nightmare. The first bedroom was empty but the next bedroom they came to was Jacob's. Jacob was lying in his bed. Police had hope for a moment that the boy was still alive but when they approached they were greeted with the worst. Jacob was in his bed with his throat slashed and stab wounds littering his body as well. There was blood all over his room including many of his toys. A toy light saber was lying in his floor; a useless object against the onslaught of the knife that had ended his life. In the master bedroom the comforter was thrown back as though the bed's occupants had left in a hurry. There was a pillow thrown awkwardly in the floor. Police wondered with horror if the boy had heard his parents being attacked before the assailant ever made it upstairs to him and clutched the pillow trying to find some comfort in the act. As they made another sweep of the house the police noticed that there were four members of the Richardson family instead of three. Instantly everyone's heart sank. A family photo depicted a sweet smiling 12 year old girl and she was nowhere to be found. Police searched that house several times over for either the body of the little girl or perhaps the girl hiding somewhere too afraid to come out after the horrible things she had witnessed but in the end they had to admit defeat, the fourth member of the Richardson family was nowhere to be seen. On the plus side her body wasn't there slain with the rest of her family but the police had to think the worst. The most logical thought was that she may have been kidnapped by whoever did this to her family. And even if she was safe, perhaps spending the night at a friend's house she would still have to deal with the tragic news that she had no family left, that her family had all been brutally attacked and killed. Hearts went out for the girl and for the family she had lost. No one wanted to be left breaking that news to a 12 year old.

The hunt for Jasmine Richardson began, or actually continued, as her parents had reported that she was missing before the terrible crime had ever even taken place. Where was Jasmine? Safe, but oblivious to the fact that this terrible thing had happened to her parents? Scared alone and possibly seriously injured in the hands of the monster that did this to her family? No one could say. As part of the investigation police visited Jasmine's school and got permission to look inside her locker. They were looking for any kind of evidence that would lead them to Jasmine whatsoever but what they found was truly a shocking discovery. When the police searched Jasmine's locker they found a hand drawn picture depicting a horrible scene. In the picture a girl's family burns to death after she puts gasoline in the sprinklers while they have a family picnic. The stick figure girl in the drawing laughs as her family burns and she escapes in her boyfriend's pickup truck. This drawing shifted suspicions entirely and Jasmine Richardson went from being searched for as a victim to being searched for as a suspect in the murder of her parents and her little brother. Consequently it didn't take the police long to track Jasmine and Jeremy down. The pair were said to be joking around with friends about the murders even at the time of apprehension. They were found at a high school in Saskatchewan only about 60 miles from Medicine Hat.

Both Jasmine and Jeremy were jailed and both were convicted. Because of Jasmine's young age at the time under Canadian law she had to be referred to as JR instead of her name. She also was protected from being tried as an adult. Although she got the maximum sentence for a child her age that sentence was only 10 years and under the conditions the time she had already spent in jail counted toward her 10 years. She ended up being imprisoned under the conditions of 4 years locked up undergoing rehabilitation and 4.5 years under very close supervision in the community. Jeremy, on the other hand, was 23 years old at the time of the murders. He was found guilty of three counts of first degree murder and sentenced to three life sentences to be served consecutively. An undercover officer rode with Jeremy while he was being transported from one facility to the other. In the conversation the two had together Jeremy expressed that he loved Jasmine more than anything and that the kind of thing he did was the kind of thing that truly expressed that love. He admitted to everything he did in such a straight forward way that it seemed he did not even grasp the gravity of the situation. He even shared his plans to marry Jasmine when they were both able to get out of prison. On murderpedia.org you can actually read the transcript of the conversation that Jeremy had with the undercover officer that he believed to be another prison being transported along with him. Steinke will be eligible for parole after 25 years.

Some of the residents of Medicine Hat were actually outraged with the outcome of the trial. They didn't think that justice would be served with Jasmine getting away with such little time. Wayne Chopek is one such resident that has spoken out about his outrage. Wayne was a friend of the family and he is disgusted at the fact that Jasmine would go free after a short ten years. However, the law remains the law and in Canada the government believes that children as young as Jasmine was at the time of the murders need to be rehabilitated rather than being locked up and having the key thrown away. They believe that such young lives have more potential value than to doom them to the rest of their lives behind bars.

Life After Murder

After Jasmine and Jeremy were arrested and jailed they still held onto the flame that was recklessly burning before the murders. They were not able to have any contact with one another except for letter writing so they wrote back and forth. This is how Jeremy came to ask Jasmine to marry him and she said yes. Below is an excerpt of the letters passed between the two when Jeremy popped the question.

Jeremy: "Without you this life isn't worth living... U said you want to get engaged? Then here's a Q...Will U marry me? If so then it is a verbal agreement!"

Jasmine: "Ahahaha! I never thought I'd find myself hystericaly laughing in a holding cell in these kinds of circumstances...or ever really. But still! ahaha you make me so happy! Yes! Yes! I will, I would love to... "

Interestingly enough as bright as that flame might have been it eventually flickered out. Although they professed the deepest of bonds neither of the two would admit to actually being the one to Kill Jacob. Both blamed the other. This was one of the deciding factors that actually showed that there were holes in the loving couple's relationship. The two broke up in jail. After incarceration the relationship that had been important enough to kill for dwindled until it was no more.

Perhaps free of any attachment to Jeremy Steinke Jasmine could truly rehabilitate. Jasmine underwent psychiatric evaluations and was determined to be suffering from oppositional defiance disorder as well as conduct disorder. When she first started therapy she was determined to suffer from dependency issues, anxiety and depression. As well as all this she was prone to immature problem solving and wishful fantasies. All this is a lot to bog down a 12 year old but was it enough of a load to excuse the execution of the murder of her entire family? Many say no, some say yes. At any rate it is indeed enough to at least explain some of her behaviors. Once in therapy Jasmine began making progress toward rehabilitation though in the beginning her details of how things played out her a bit skewed to reality. By 2010 Jasmine was making significant progress in her rehabilitation and had professed to be sorry for the crimes she committed. As the terms of her sentencing were laid out she got credit on her sentence for the time she spent in jail awaiting trial and then after 4 years of incarceration she was deemed fit enough to go into the community under very close supervision for 4.5 years. During that time Jasmine was shown to exhibit exemplary behavior as well as being a straight A student. Jasmine was admitted to Calgary University where she continued to earn really high grades. This year, 2016, in May Jasmine became a completely free woman. The courts have no reason to think that she is a danger to society any longer. It's been a decade and she has been through extensive amounts of therapy and shown nothing but progress in that entire time.

A very interesting thing to look at here is the chemistry between Jasmine and Jeremy. One asks themselves, was the combination just toxic? Would either of them been capable of doing something like this on their own? It seems that the pairing of the two and the dependency that both of them exhibited for the other was actual such an explosive combination that it pushed them over the edge just enough to create the perfect circumstance for this to happen. Jasmine has said that she wasn't really being serious when she would send Jeremy messages saying that she had a plan to kill her parents and live with him. That she didn't really mean to go through with it when she joked about murdering her family or made drawings depicting their deaths. But she felt those feelings and she told Jeremy. Steinke just happened to be easily manipulated, a regular user of multiple drugs, and even believed himself to be a 300 year old werewolf. Jeremy and Jasmine both took the dark Goth culture they lived within to the extreme. They exchanged vials of blood and Jeremy wore one around his neck. When the two were faced with Jasmine's parents making them unable to see one another dark fantasies were transformed into evil realities. Perhaps the fantasies that both harbored were purely fantasies until the tension kept rising and rising and the two kept feeding off of each other until the combination of each of their dark thoughts breathed life into the other. In the end it doesn't really matter to ask if either would have been capable of the atrocity on their own because it wasn't the case that they were on their own. They were bound together by an obsessive unhealthy love and the obsessive unhealthy thoughts in both their heads took form in reality. The result was unspeakable horror.

That late April day three lives were lost much too soon and in such a violent way that it is nearly unthinkable. That alone is enough to make this tragedy stand out forever in history but that's not all that was lost. Little Gareth will never be the same. Though he is a successful high schooler now the memory of those bodies and the memory of the loss of his best friend will always be with him. And of course Jasmine Richardson and Jeremy Steinke's lives will forever be changed and affected. Jeremy will most likely spend his entire life in jail having had only 23 short years of freedom. Parole will be an unlikely event. Even though Jasmine has improved and rehabilitated, even if she successfully integrates back into society, she will forever have this as a part of her past. She will also forever have people that look at her as a monster. Her story is known all over the world. Jasmine is the youngest person in Canada to have ever committed such a heinous crime. It is a question to ponder as to whether Jasmine has forgiven herself or if she is forever haunted by the monster that she perhaps did not even know lurked inside her. Perhaps even scarier to think of is the possibility that she really could live without being constantly haunted by the crime. Is there any amount of rehabilitation that should erase that guilt? And then one has to consider Jeremy. Has he come to terms with the events? Is he sorry for his crimes? Will a life in prison in any way begin to repay his debt for those three lives that he so brutally extinguished?

Life in Medicine Hat continues on. It is still a relatively safe place to live. Medicine Hat is still a relatively small tight knit place filled with working class suburbs. There are still nice neighborhoods that feel safe the way that Ross Glen did before tragedy came to town but no one will forget what could happen no matter how nice or normal a family might seem they will know that a tragedy like this could happen to any family because it already has.

GIRL MONSTER : THE TRUE STORY OF BROOKEY LEE WEST

SARAH SANCHEZ

Brookey Lee West

One of the most gruesome and bizarre crimes that ever occurred in Las Vegas was discovered on February 5, 2001. The manager of Canyon Gate Mini Storage, Bill Unruh, opened Unit #317 after someone reported a very bad smell.

He found a 45-gallon garbage container that had a brownish liquid oozing out of it at the bottom. He called police.

Detectives entered a unit that contained normal items on one side and the oozing sealed-up garbage container on the other side. There were also books about witchcraft and Satanism in the locker.

Unruh told police that the unit had been rented in the names of Brookey Lee West and Christine Smith on June 26, 1998.

The garbage container had been made airtight with duct tape, packing tape, plastic wrap, and garbage bags. The leakage was coming from a hole that had developed in the bottom.

When investigators cut the container open, more fluid seeped out accompanied by dead maggots. They could see a human body inside, very decomposed. The body was mostly liquefied, but those on scene could easily see that a white plastic bag was tied around the person's face.

Crime scene analysts tested the brownish liquid for human blood and the test was positive.

In the storage unit, Detective David Mesinar found Christine Smith's wallet, ID, prescriptions, and documents relating to her Social Security payments.

Dental records confirmed that the body was Christine's. Christine would have been 68 years old if she was still alive.

Detectives began by looking for Christine's daughter, 46-year-old Brookey Lee West.

Brookey is now serving life without parole for murdering her mother. Brookey may also have murdered her brother Travis and probably murdered her third husband Howard.

Brookey's mother Christine, her father Leroy, her husband Howard, Brookey herself, and Brookey's brother Travis all had tragic childhoods and went on to live destructive or self-destructive lives.

On hearing this story, some might be amazed that nobody killed Christine before she reached her 60s. By all accounts, she was a sociopathic parasite who had never worked a day in her life other than her short degrading stint as a prostitute at the age of sixteen.

By the time her daughter killed her, though, she was a harmless pain in the ass with major health problems and suffering from dementia.

Christine's Childhood

Christine Merle Sands was born on February 14, 1932, in Ennis, Ellis County, Texas. Her parents were Clyde and Annie Sands. As it was for many people during the Great Depression, life was a struggle.

Ennis was a hub for the cotton industry, and Clyde worked as a long haul trucker moving cotton products. He also worked as a lineman installing power lines across the country. The lineman job was very demanding physically, but it paid well when the work was available. Even with both jobs, money was always tight.

Clyde's work often took him away from home for long periods leaving Annie to run the home.

Annie was a housewife and a loving woman. The Sands were not abusive parents, but day-to-day life didn't allow them the time or capacity to nurture their six children.

Trudy was born in 1911. She was followed by Woodrow, Lawrence, Richard Bob, Billy, and finally Christine in 1932.

The two youngest children, Billy and Christine, made it to the eighth grade before they dropped out of school. Their parents had no concept of the importance of education, so this was not an issue in the family.

Christine later told Brookey that a family member had begun molesting her at the age of eight. Billy knows nothing about this, but such a thing would not have been talked about within a family in 1930s Texas.

Billy does say that Christine was a good girl who started to spin out of control around the age of ten.

When she dropped out of school, Christine was thirteen years old. By sixteen, she had gone off the rails. Says Billy, "I think, personally, she was restless at home by herself . . . she was looking for anything that come along so she could grab a hold of it and get out of little old Ennis."

At sixteen, Christine married a young man. This is how Billy describes him: "He was a bad character. I don't know what in the world she ever seen in him, because he was really something . . . It was bad from the word go. Several people said he treated her like a dog."

Christine and her new husband ran off to Houston. According to Billy's wife JoAnn, the husband was very abusive. Very soon, he had turned her out as a Houston whore. Christine felt degraded and she was very angry. She got her daddy to come and take her back to Ennis.

Leroy's Childhood

Leroy was born in Russia. When he was a baby, his family moved to the U.S. and settled in the hills of Tennessee.

His parents' marriage was violent. His father murdered his mother during a domestic dispute. According to West, "He cut her head off with a machete in Tennessee . . . my dad said his father went to prison for about ten years." Leroy was five at the time.

Leroy's older sisters pinned a note to his jacket explaining that he was an orphan and put him on a bus. He ended up alone on a city street corner. The woman who found him gave him to another woman, an alcoholic who was unable to have children. She and her husband thought that being childless made them look bad so they took him in.

His new parents, named Smith, took him to Arkansas and named him Leroy.

Leroy told his own family later that much of his time as a member of the Smith family was spent living in tents and shacks.

At sixteen, determined to get away from that family, he lied about his age and enlisted in the army. His love of guns began in the army. He also liked the military discipline and the structure it imposed.

By then he was already defensive, antisocial, reclusive, filled with anger, and very racist.

West said about her father, "My dad didn't like nothing that wasn't white. That's just the way he was. I used to tell him, 'You know what, Dad? If you tried to join the skinheads, you would be president of them in six months.' He would be like, 'Yeah, I would be.'"

Leroy & Christine

Leroy Smith was stationed at Fort Bliss in El Paso, Texas, when he met Christine Sands in 1947. It's not clear what she was doing in El Paso, 600 miles from Ennis.

She was sixteen, freshly out of her disastrous first marriage. She had blue eyes, long blond hair, and a sexy figure in a tight dress. He was eighteen and looked very fine in his army uniform. They had a lust-hate relationship from the start. They were both infatuated, but his arrogance ticked her off. Her attitude ticked him off but it also made him want her.

They dated on his weekends off. It was casual for him, but she was not going to let this handsome army guy out of her grasp. Soon Christine was "pregnant."

According to Brookey, "My dad said that's why he married her. He told me he wanted to divorce her after he was married to her for about three months. He said, 'I knew I'd been had.'"

Leroy As A Cop – Leroy Gets Into Drugs

Shortly after the marriage, Leroy left the army and was hired as a patrol officer with the El Paso Police Department. El Paso was crawling with drug dealers, drug smugglers, pimps, and prostitutes in the early 1950s. Whatever his motives may have been when he signed up, Leroy soon dove into the muck.

"This is when my father started using drugs, and this is also about the time my mom started using drugs, too," Brookey says.

Leroy told West that he made extra money by shaking down drug dealers. "He'd take dope from some suspect and give it to some snitch to sell it to somebody."

Leroy's drug of preference was speed. He started taking it because he needed energy when he was on night shift, but soon he was popping pills every day. Being a crooked cop in a city full of Mexican-American criminals was right up Leroy's racist alley.

According to Brookey, "It was getting to the point where he was getting really violent. My dad wouldn't back down from anybody, and he had a real bad temper."

At this time, Christine was also doing drugs and beginning to behave strangely. She began to lie all the time and for no reason. One of her favorite lies was that she was Cherokee. Sometimes she was Apache. According to Chloe Smith, Leroy's second wife, this drove Leroy crazy as he thought of Native Americans as "savages."

The couple's life was out of control before they were even twenty years old, before their children were born.

Leroy cheated on Christine constantly. As a cop, he had a lot of access. Leroy later told Chloe Smith that he didn't even try to hide it from Christine because she wasn't interested in sex anyway. He also thought Christine was crazy.

While Leroy was at work, shaking down drug dealers and getting it on with prostitutes, Christine was either in the bars downtown or sitting in the apartment smoking, drinking, and popping pills.

They were fighting constantly and violently by 1951. One time, Christine, in a drunken stupor, crawled into bed, put a gun to Leroy's head, and pulled the trigger. There were no bullets in the gun so she put it under her pillow and went to sleep. Leroy later told Brookey that he had awakened when Christine entered the room and, knowing the gun was empty, pretended to be still asleep.

Brookey Lee West: "Who knows why? But my mother didn't really need a reason to kill anybody. My mother was a very devious person."

Leroy & Christine Pregnant

In 1952, Leroy decided to leave and move on with his life. That's when Christine announced that she was pregnant.

Leroy later told his second wife, "She never got pregnant, she never got pregnant, never got pregnant. Then, when the pressure was on, suddenly it happened."

Eventually it was obvious that she was telling the truth about being pregnant, but Leroy always wondered if Brookey was really his child.

Brookey Is Born

Brookey Lee Smith was born in an El Paso hospital on June 28, 1953. Both parents fell in love with her sweet nature, brown hair, and hazel eyes. As a toddler, she loved her parents and all she cared about was pleasing them.

When Christine took time off from partying, she took Brookey to Aunt Trudy's house or to the park to play. But both of her parents were drug addicts and alcoholics, so Brookey was often left home alone.

Travis Is Born

In 1956, Christine was pregnant again.

West says, "My dad was furious with her . . . 'You just did this to put another rope around my neck!' I heard that for years."

Travis Lee Smith was born August 29, 1956. West recollects, "My brother was a chubby, heavy baby. They put these striped shirts on him, and he looked like a wrestler."

Unlike Brookey, Travis was a problem child from the start. West thinks he may have had ADHD: "He would chew on Sheetrock . . . he was something else. He was like my mother in that he did not have a good disposition. Him and my mother adored each other."

Little Travis was born with a tongue that was too long for his mouth. This made it difficult for him to nurse from a bottle and he had a speech impediment most of his life. People thought he was slow, but he wasn't. They couldn't understand the language he had made up for himself.

Travis was a biter as a tot, and his mother encouraged him to bite people and children. The other kids called him "the snapping turtle."

Brookey & Travis' Early Life

Family snapshots show that the early lives of Brookey and Travis were not total hell. Their smiles in the pictures show that they had some fun times with their parents. But most of the time they were lonely and abandoned.

Brookey made paper dolls and dressed them up as fantasy queens or princesses. She recalls that she only had one birthday party, because her parents were too busy partying to put it together most years. She looked after Travis for days at a time while her parents were out barhopping.

West says, "We had all kinds of medications in our cabinets. Speed, then tranquilizers to calm [them] down." Her mother told her years later that they were both too strung out to be decent parents.

Leroy Is Fired & The Smiths Move To California

In the mid-1950s, Leroy was fired from the police department. He told Brookey and others that it was because he had borrowed money from the police department – which was apparently a normal thing – but didn't return it as per SOP.

Chloe, Leroy's second wife, thinks that it was something worse than that. Leaving the El Paso PD was a sore topic with him when he met her more than twenty years later. Considering his activities as a cop – shaking down drug dealers, getting snitches to sell drugs for him, and using prostitutes as his personal harem – Chloe may well be right.

In 1959, the Smiths headed west. They stayed in cheap motels in New Mexico and Ventura, California, before they chose to settle in Bakersfield, California.

Bakersfield was an oil city full of Texans and Oklahomans who had migrated there during the Depression. It was a honky-tonk town and Leroy and Christine totally belonged.

Leroy found a steady job putting down carpet in houses and was able to rent a home in a low-income neighborhood.

Brookey describes the neighborhood: "Most of them are just like my parents. Alcoholics, drinkers, partiers, sitting out in front of their homes drinking and working on some old wrecked-out car, saying, 'Go in the house there, baby, and get daddy a beer! Go in there and get me my shotgun!' They'd all be out there shouting at each other in the yard with their rifles pointed at each other."

Leroy and Christine partied hard in the Bakersfield bar scene. Brookey, seven, had to look after Travis, four. Sometimes for two to three days at a stretch.

During work hours, Leroy laid carpet while Christine spent all day in bed recovering. She always had aches and pains. But when Leroy came home and wanted to go out, Christine was ready to party.

How Leroy managed to spend his days laying carpet is hard to guess. He popped amphetamines and tranquilizers, and he drank wine all the time. He didn't seem to care about what booze and drugs might be doing to him.

The Smith Family Goes Downhill In Bakersfield

West described the next step in her parents' spiral: "That's about the time when my parents started going to doctors to get more and more pills. They were writing prescriptions for my parents for painkillers, and then my parents would sell them. Sell them to their friends or whoever wanted them . . . that's how they made their money."

She added, "I took care of them and all their problems. If I could hide something for them, I did. If they told me to lie, I lied. Someone would call up and say, 'Can I speak to your dad?' And I'd say, 'Well, he's not here. He went to a doctor.' Meanwhile, my dad was right there smashed out of his mind."

Around this time, Leroy's drunken rages sometimes became so violent that his spankings left bruises on their bottoms in the shape of his hand. According to West. "There were times that he would spank us with a two-by-four. I'd go to school with bruises all over, but no one ever said anything."

The house was full of guns. They were even underneath the beds and the cushions of the couch. Leroy also carried a gun.

He once threatened to kill a man who was driving too fast in their neighborhood.

He told the guy after pulling him out of his car, "You see all these kids around here? If you want to run over somebody's kid, make sure you run over somebody else's, because if you run over one of my kids, I'm going to twist your head off your shoulders and use it as a doorknob."

Christine was a screamer rather than a hitter. Brookey was afraid of both of them and learned to be careful. Brookey and Travis were treated the way their parents had been treated as children. As objects.

The alcohol, drugs, neglect, arguments, and violence damaged both children emotionally.

Added to that stress on the children, their parents kept splitting up and getting back together. There was constant talk of divorce. Christine would disappear for days and then

Leroy would disappear for days. The children couldn't help thinking that everything was their fault.

Leroy & Christine Break Up – Christine Shoots Her Lover & Goes To Prison

In 1961, Leroy left Christine for a waitress named Faye. He moved Brookey and Travis into Faye's house with Faye's six kids.

Meanwhile, Christine hooked up with a married man. He worked as a mason. They had a steamy romance for a few months. He promised her they would have a new life together somewhere.

According to Christine, they had been planning to kill his wife with "sleeping medicine, a lot of sleeping stuff."

Christine told police in a taped admission: "He wanted me to kill her, and I thought, 'You son of a bitch, if I killed her, where would I be with you?' Who would he get to kill me? That's the way I felt about it."

In the early weeks of 1961, the man told Christine he was going back to his wife. She was angry. She told police later, "I said, 'Well, you know, you can take me to the water, you son of a bitch, but ain't going to drown me because I'll kill your ass.'"

On January 24, 1961, Christine asked the man and his wife to meet her at a bar in Bakersfield to help her plan how to get her own marriage back on track. She showed up at 7:30 p.m. as arranged. She had a sawed-off 16-guage shotgun on her lap, hidden by her jacket and sweater.

The couple showed up a few minutes later and sat down. Christine reached under the table, pulled the trigger, and shot him.

The man, aged thirty, was rushed to a hospital with blood pouring out of him. His arm had been shattered, but his life was saved through surgery.

Christine, aged twenty-eight, was taken away in handcuffs. She later told police, "I didn't have the least feeling of sympathy. Hell, no." In fact, she bragged about it for the rest of her life. She also told police at the time that she did not know where Brookey and Travis were living.

Life During Christine's Trial

Leroy's relationship with Faye was falling apart. He took Brookey and Travis back to live in Christine's home while they waited for Christine's day in court.

Brookey found this time very traumatic. She was only eight, and her mother's crime was on the television news. She was very ashamed of her mother.

West remembers going with her father to visit her mother in jail and at the trial: "My dad took a dress down to her, and it was a honky-tonk dress with no back, so her lawyers put a sweater around her because they didn't want her in court in that thing. They wrote in the paper that she was a Lolita."

In March 1961, Christine was sent to the California Institute for Women (CIA) with a sentence of fourteen years for assault with intent to commit murder.

Brookey later said, "My mother talked about that shooting like she was some sort of movie star. The first thing out of her mouth about it was, 'Well, you know, I went to prison because I shot that son of a bitch. He deserved it.'"

Christine In Prison

Christine fit in well with the people in prison. She had always been a manipulative person and knew how to connect with people. She worked it there too. As a kitchen worker, she sneaked extra sweets to certain inmates. Some were outraged when she was moved out of kitchen duty to another job.

Brookey & Travis After Christine Is Sent To Prison

Brookey, aged eight, didn't fare well after all of this. She couldn't pay attention in school. She didn't talk about her situation to friends or teachers. She failed second grade.

Travis, aged five, was completely traumatized. Leroy told Brookey to be an adult and tell Travis that his mother was dead and buried. If she was to be treated as an adult, she should act like one. She did what she was told.

Within a year of Christine being in prison, Leroy and the kids lived in Fresno, then Oregon, then San Luis Obispo, and ended up back in Bakersfield.

As Brookey describes it, they were always worried, they were always moving, there was always trauma. She says of her dad, "Drink all day and half the night. It was getting to where he couldn't even work anymore. We were living in another run-down motel, and he was feeding us crackers for dinner. Pillar to post and motel to motel. If you didn't have something to eat that day, you asked the neighbors for something."

Orphanage

In 1962, Leroy decided that the children would be better off without him. His drinking was more important than looking after them, maybe. They had not heard from their mother since she'd gone to prison.

He dropped them off at the Sunnycrest Home for Youths in Bakersfield. Brookey was screaming that she would be good if he let them come home.

As it turned out, Brookey and Travis loved the orphanage. They went to school regularly, they got good grades, they were properly fed, and they had clothes to wear. The place was run by a loving older couple.

Travis, in particular, became attached to the couple. Brookey did not miss her parents. Both of them would have loved to stay there forever.

Christine Gets Out Of Jail, The Smiths Move To San Jose

One day, Leroy showed up at the orphanage with Christine in the car. She had been paroled after serving only two years of her sentence. She had five years of probation to go yet. Travis cried and screamed – he did not want to leave the orphanage. But leave he did.

Brookey Lee West's take on this is that her parents "sought each other out after my mom got out of prison because it was one of those types of relationships, like when an abused woman keeps going back to her husband. They didn't want each other, but then, when they were apart, they really did. And then, they didn't want each other again. That's the way their relationship was. On and off all the time."

San Jose

In 1965, the family moved to San Jose, now known as Silicone Valley. Any stability the children had enjoyed at the orphanage was gone forever now. Christine was back in their lives and San Jose was where Leroy would dedicate himself to Satan.

Leroy got another job laying carpet and rented a house on Lafayette Street, a mostly Hispanic neighborhood.

Brookey, as a white kid, didn't fit in. She played alone or with her brother.

She says, "The kids weren't very friendly to me. I was always big for my age, and by the time I was twelve, I was tall. I didn't look twelve, and I didn't look like everyone else."

Travis, only nine, was self-destructive and he was fighting. "My brother started using drugs when he was nine," Brookey says. "Pills right out of the cabinet. The bathroom cabinet couldn't hold all these pills. Any color you wanted."

Leroy Embraces Satanism

The family had a friend who lived about six blocks away that West only knows as "Mrs. Beauford." Leroy was especially close to her.

One day, Brookey, aged thirteen, was sent there by her mother to return a borrowed dish. "I knocked on her door, the door sort of came open and I said hello, and nobody answered. I stood there for a second, and I hear this moaning, groaning, kind of like screaming. It's coming from the basement."

When she went to the back of the house, she saw a bunch of people doing a spell or something.

Leroy got into the spells and witchcraft quickly. The idea of making enemies suffer was enticing to him. By the late 1960s he was a regular participant in the ceremonies with all the candles, robes, and chants that anyone might imagine.

Of course, none of this was unusual in California in the 1960s and 1970s. But Leroy started to believe that he was a warlock with a high rank in Satan's legion.

West's take on this: "He had books, knives and other stuff. They wore their robes, almost like the Ku Klux Klan, and it was a secretive organization . . . My dad identified with that stuff. He didn't go around killing people, but he believed Satan was the ruler of this world, and he could give you anything you wanted. You just have to know how to get in touch."

West claims that she understands all of this, has read a lot about it, that it is valid, and that true believers can actually cast spells that work. She says she has not practiced it herself but knows of people in very high positions who do.

Brookey In High School

At the age of fourteen, Brookey was attending Santa Clara High School in Jan Jose. By this time she was very attractive. She had hazel eyes, curly brown hair, a shapely body, and gorgeous legs from doing ballet. She wore the same type of clothes her mom had worn in the Bakersfield honky-tonk days.

West: "I dressed very sexy. I was a looker. The boys all wanted a date with me, but I didn't want to go. I was very standoffish about men. Probably because of the way my home life was, I couldn't invite anybody home."

She had lower than average grades, she was aimless, and she had no plans.

Smith Family Late 1960s

In the late 1960s, Leroy wasn't trying to hide his affairs. He was also drinking very heavily. Christine was fed up and moved out. The resulting divorce was traumatic for Brookey and Travis.

Travis simply dropped out of school to do drugs. It was all he cared about ever again, really. He loved speed and meth. He didn't want to work, though Leroy tried to get him involved in the carpet laying job. He lied and stole to get drugs and was always in legal trouble.

Christine, after years of doing drugs and booze all day every day, joined Alcoholics Anonymous and was eventually successful at quitting both.

She joined a church and got Brookey to attend services with her. She wanted to understand all the traumas of her life, the molestation, being turned into a hooker by her first husband, why she married so young in the first place. Christine wanted to find God. Soon she was able to talk a good game about Jesus but, according to West, she wanted to be forgiven without putting in the work.

Christine was still full of spite and anger.

West explains: "My mom started going to church with me when I was in my teens, but she still viewed religion as a matter of convenience. She wasn't book smart enough to learn the Bible, or even read it, and she didn't apply herself."

Christine Is Actually Crazy

Christine had always experienced aches and pains, she always had a cough, she was always sick in bed. Even with her lifestyle – the smoking, drinking, and drugs – these problems were deemed psychosomatic and she was referred to a mental health clinic.

During her screening, she beat the doctor on the head with the heel of her boot. Authorities ordered her to see a state psychiatrist, Sydney Goldstein. She was a patient of his for the next ten years.

During one visit, Goldstein's receptionist told Brookey that Goldstein only took the sickest of patients. That's when Brookey first understood that Christine was seriously mentally ill.

She had an opportunity to snoop her mother's medical file, and in it she read that her mother was a "sociopath with psychopathic tendencies." Sociopaths care for nobody but themselves.

When discussing this eye-opener, West said, "She was a total sociopath."

Brookey Launches Out On Her Own

Brookey Lee Smith graduated from Santa Clara High School in 1971. It was time to get away from her insane mother, her Satanist warlock racist father, and her dropout druggy brother.

Her grades were lower than average, but she was accepted into the army. The army was not what she had imagined it to be. All the rules and restrictions seemed stupid to her. After nine months, she managed to get out honorably. She had wanted to be a spy.

She was broke and had no post-secondary education. At twenty years old, she was living with Christine, paying all the bills by working odd jobs, waitress jobs, legal secretary jobs. Christine had no job and Brookey desperately wanted to get away from her.

1973 – Brookey Has A Daughter

In 1973, Brookey met a man at the church she and her mother had been attending. Soon they were dating. He was handsome and smooth-talking. She considered him the love of her life.

Ronald Ray Veramontes "was good-looking, he was charming, so we dated for a while," says West. "We dated maybe six or seven months, and I was wild about him. I was in love with him. Completely gone."

Veramontes later told police that their relationship had never been serious.

Brookey got pregnant during a weekend trip to Los Angeles. "I just told him I was pregnant, straight up, and it was over the phone, because he called me to see how I was feeling. That's when he gave me this snotty-assed remark, saying, 'How do you know it's mine?' I'm naïve up to this point. I think I knew in my heart he was already out seeing other women on the side, but I really couldn't face that. As soon as I told him I was pregnant, he was gone," she said.

Brookey's parents were furious. "They called me all kinds of names. Bitch, whore, slut, a tramp. 'Why don't you have an abortion?'"

In 1974, at O'Connor Catholic Hospital, Brookey gave birth to a beautiful girl.

1977 – First Marriage Fizzles

Around 1977, Brookey saw a classified ad looking for a female singer for a country band. She was twenty-four and it sounded like a way to make some extra cash. The ad had been placed by a fifty-eight-year-old concert promoter who was an Okie to boot. He was infatuated with her and they were married within a few months.

"He was real good to me at first," she says. "The one thing I always thought was real good about him was he never tried to hit me, never tried to raise his hand toward me, even though we had some nasty arguments. That's the good things I can say about him. But he had drinking issues, dope issues, same thing all my husbands had. I guess it was the caretaker syndrome."

She sang in the band for a while. "You have to be drunk to sing that stuff," she said later.

She wasn't into singing in the band. After about six weeks, she said to him, "Who the hell are you? What do I want with you? This is just not working." They divorced.

1981 – Career In Silicon Valley Takes Off, Second Marriage Fizzles

Brookey eventually got a decent job as a security guard at National Advanced Systems, a computer company located in Palo Alto. Soon she became a secretary there, a much better job, and that is how she met her second husband "West."

She took some papers to his office. He asked her out. They became engaged during their first date and were married within five months. Brookey was twenty-eight and he was forty-nine.

According to Brookey's description, "He was tall, slender, very Norwegian, with sharp features. Good-looking, blond haired."

Christine didn't approve of Brookey marrying a man so much older. Mr. West though Christine was crazy and mean. They couldn't stand each other. They constantly fought. This marriage was also over within months.

Brookey blames her bipolar disorder for both of those marriages. She wasn't stable then, she says. She has a hatred for West that she doesn't have for her first husband.

She says that West molested her daughter during a school vacation. "If I would have had a reason to kill somebody, it would have probably been him. If I wanted to kill him for money, it would have been ideal, because he had $250,000 in life insurance," she says.

Before the divorce, she was set to inherit his estate if he died. "He signed everything over to me in case of his death, so if I had a reason to kill somebody, it would have been him."

Brookey Wants To Give Her Daughter Away

Brookey was working long hours as a legal secretary to support her mother and daughter. When the child was four, Brookey sent her to a boarding school in Arizona so she would not have to be left alone with crazy Christine. There weren't a lot of visits back and forth.

By the time her daughter was nine, around 1983, Brookey decided she wanted her daughter to stay with the people who ran the school. Brookey had mood swings. She was unstable. She did not think she could be a good parent.

But her daughter's father, Ray Veramontes, refused to give up his parental rights. He wanted to adopt her rather than let her be given away.

West was furious with him and so was Leroy. No Mexican was going to tell his daughter what to do.

According to Veramontes, "I wanted to have custody of my daughter, full custody. It was not up for conversation with them. It wasn't in their heads."

Veramontes Receives Witchy Threats

On January 14, 1985, a man dressed in black showed up at Veramontes' grandmother's house asking for "Ray." One witness said the man was wearing a Halloween mask. He shot her in the chest with a .22. With surgery, she survived.

On February 13, Veramontes received a handwritten letter with a pentagram drawn on it and satanic chants threatening the murder of his entire family. "You pray to your God, I'll pray to mine. We'll see whose God is stronger," it said.

He knew that Leroy was a warlock or a witch. Veramontes was terrified of what Leroy might do and gave up his custody battle. His daughter was adopted by the teachers in Arizona.

Brookey's Tech Writing Career

While working at National Advanced Systems, Brookey was promoted from her secretary position to working with hardware and mainframes. She was also studying everything she could find about programming, engineering, and troubleshooting. She was drawn to technical writing and turned out to be extremely good at it.

By the late 1980s and early 1990s, she was doing technical writing on contract for the best companies in Silicon Valley – including Sun, Intel, and Cisco – earning $65-$100 per hour.

She bought a house in Los Banos, wore expensive clothes, and drove a Jaguar.

But she still had Christine around her neck.

Brookey's Life With Christine

Christine was living with Brookey and living off Brookey. They lived together in a rental house in San Jose in the early 1990s before Brookey bought the house in Los Banos. Brookey was kept on her toes just trying to make sure her mother didn't do anything crazy.

Christine tried to poison a neighbor's dog with cayenne pepper and then with gopher poison. When Brookey asked her about it, Christine said, "Yeah, I did. I hate that son of a bitch." The dog survived.

Though they were always fighting, they also loved each other. Brookey had absorbed Christine's obsession with Native American culture. Now they were both claiming Native American roots, and they loved shopping for Indian jewelry and art.

Leroy Post-Christine: Chloe

Leroy's second wife, Chloe, had been through two failed marriages by 1975. She had two children from her first marriage. They were living with their father. She met Leroy while she was working at a tavern near Santa Clara University.

Chloe was born in Massachusetts. Her alcoholic father moved the family to rural Arizona in the 1940s. Their life was "pretty desolate and pretty awful."

Leroy was affectionate and protective. He made her feel special. They were married in 1977 and she hoped this marriage would be different.

They rented a house on Lawrence Street in San Jose. Leroy was still working as a carpet layer. Women still made him "sparkle and twinkle." He was still a hostile person who did not trust people. But he loved Chloe unconditionally and thrived on her stable nature. Chloe was so unlike Christine.

He came with a lot of baggage. He was always falling off the wagon. He was still a raging racist. He had guns hidden all over the house. During arguments, he would threaten to do to Chloe what his father had done to his mother.

During the twenty years they were married, Leroy explored a variety of religions. Chloe never saw Leroy engaged in any kind of devil worship, though in hindsight she can think of a couple of instances.

On one occasion, his Mexican neighbors had been parking in front of his house and he left them a satanic note similar to the one that Veramontes had received. He had an excuse for that – Mexicans are very religious and using religious stuff is a good way to get under their skin.

Another time, after Brookey and Christine had dropped off some furniture and Leroy was putting it in the garage, Chloe saw him sealing a grotesque Halloween mask into a cabinet or a wall. He said it belonged to Brookey and Christine.

She loved him and he was a good husband. He took over all the housework when she went back to school to get a business degree. He was kind and considerate. He wasn't drinking *all* the time.

He had one rule only: Chloe should never associate with Christine because Christine was crazy. She should keep Brookey at a distance too. Chloe would have liked to get together with Leroy's ex-wife and children for holidays, but Leroy explained that they were crazy and not good people.

Whenever Brookey or Travis showed up to discuss something with Leroy, they walked past Chloe, straight into Leroy's office as if Chloe didn't exist.

Only after twenty years of marriage did Chloe see Leroy's frightening side.

Travis Post-Childhood

Chloe did have some contact with Travis. He was not as *persona non grata* as Christine and Brookey were.

Travis was tall and large with long, bushy black hair. He was incapable of holding a job and was often homeless due to his drug addiction.

Chloe: "I don't think he even graduated from the seventh grade. He started using drugs very young, and I think he burned himself out. He did poorly in school, and I just don't think he was very smart. He didn't get it."

Leroy was always trying to help Travis. Brookey could take care of herself but Travis could not. Leroy bought him vehicles, got him flooring jobs, found him apartments. But Travis was too busy partying to take advantage of any of the help.

Leroy started his own flooring business in San Jose – Smith's Floor Covering – so he could hand it over to Travis at some point. Leroy shut it down within a few months and started doing security work.

In the early 1980s, Travis hit bottom. He was in his late twenties or early thirties. He lived on drugs and booze and on the streets. He ate one meal a day at a soup kitchen. He was arrested at least ten times in a period of seven years for public intoxication, loitering, drug related offenses, arson, and attacking an ex-girlfriend during a meth trip.

Brookey West: "My brother liked speed, meth, and he had some guns. He and a friend went over to this gal's house, and they broke in, and she was in bed with this other guy.

So my brother strips them all down naked, and he goes in another room, and he gets this woman's little boy, and he brings him back in, and he says, 'Now you see what a whore your mother is?'"

Someone heard the commotion and called 911. Travis landed in jail.

Brookey continues the story, "By the time he calms down in jail, his hand is broke, his nose is broke, and they were like, what do you expect? So he was going to go to prison for a long time."

He didn't though. Travis was diagnosed as a schizophrenic, judged criminally insane, and sent to Atascadero State Hospital at San Luis Obispo.

Chloe and Leroy visited him there one Christmas. Chloe brought cookies that she had baked for him.

"He came across as a big guy with all this hair," she said, "but to me he just seemed like this big, harmless woolly bear."

Travis cried when Chloe hugged him.

When he was released, Travis went back to the streets. Leroy continued to try to help him get work, but Travis was physically disabled because of his years of doing drugs. At that point, all Leroy could do for him was set up a bank account so Travis could receive his disability checks.

In the early 1990s, Leroy tried one last time to convince Travis to get off the streets and come home. "Dad, I don't want you coming down here anymore," Travis said. "I like living on the street. I've got lots of friends. When you come down here, you just bother me, you disturb me. I don't want you coming down here anymore. I want you to leave me alone."

Christine's Love Life Post-Leroy

In the early 1980s, Christine, now in her early fifties, wanted a man. She came on to workmen and other men, but was always rebuffed. They found her weird. That must have been distressing for someone who had always been so desirable to men.

She honed in on her chiropractor, successful and divorced.

She made a pornographic audio tape of herself masturbating and panting about her love for him. It sounds like a tape intended for someone already involved in a physical relationship with the sender. But the doctor was not remotely interested in Christine.

At one point in the tape, she interrupts the porn for twenty minutes to include a speech from her favorite televangelist who was on TV celebrating the Fourth of July.

According to West, Christine had become obsessed with religious imagery by this time.

After the sermon, Christine's tape goes back to moaning and groaning. She begs the doctor for a secret place for the two of them to be together.

Christine didn't end up giving the tape to the chiropractor because his secretary told her about some other woman the doctor was in love with. The relationship had existed only in Christine's mind, but she was very angry with him.

She told Brookey, "I'm going to get me a gun, and I'm going to shoot that son of a bitch, just like I shot that other one." Brookey refused to get her a gun.

Mother & Daughter Shoplifting Team

Christine and Brookey were caught a few times shoplifting blouses, scarves, and jewelry from high-end department stores. They worked it as a team.

In 1985, Brookey was caught and pleaded guilty to misdemeanor theft and paid a fine. Later that year, when they were arrested after shoplifting together, Christine was upset that the police found Brookey's arrest record but did not find Christine's own conviction record. So she bragged to them about having shot a man.

Mother and daughter were convicted of burglary and conspiracy and sentenced to thirty days in jail and two years of probation.

1993 – Brookey's Third Husband, Howard

In late 1993, Christine and Brookey went to an A.A. meeting at the San Jose Indian Center. Brookey was wearing trampy clothes and Elvira-ish makeup, looking like she wanted to cause trouble. Christine dished out her alcoholic stories and her prison stories and thumped the bible a bit. When the meeting was almost over, Brookey went on a tirade about her ex (West) and how he deserved to be dead.

Everybody at the meeting was afraid of Brookey. Nobody believed the two were Native American.

Later that year, Brookey took up with a man from the Native rehab house next to the Indian Center, Wayne Ike.

Ike said, "She wanted to marry an Indian guy." He loved the sex. But he sensed something was wrong with her. For example, why was this prosperous woman hanging out at a Native rehab center?

Ike also didn't like what she said about kids – she didn't like them and she had given her daughter away. He didn't like how she always talked about money. And he didn't like it when she pulled a gun on him and said, "If I ever catch you messing around, I'll use this on you. If I catch you fucking around, I'll shoot your ass."

Once Ike decided that West was crazy, he hid whenever she came around.

In 1994, Brookey changed her focus to a different man at the halfway house, Howard Simon St. John. She had a good job, a nice car, and a nice house. Howard was a homeless drunk and a drug addict.

Howard's Background

Howard was a child of the South Dakota Sioux, a very noble tribe. He was born on May 15, 1958. He'd had some childhood traumas and been ostracized by his family. He had been drinking regularly since the age of sixteen. His family moved back and forth between South Dakota and California a few times. The last time they left California, Howard dropped out of high school and stayed in California.

He loved partying and he loved booze. He was talented at tweaking cars and often worked for his friend Tony Mercado as a mechanic.

During his mid-twenties, Howard drank until he was unconscious every day. He could down a bottle of tequila. He was also getting into cocaine. He was living on the streets. He already had a huge beer belly and rotten teeth.

By 1988, Howard, aged thirty, was about as low as anybody can go. He'd been arrested for drunk driving, assault and battery, public intoxication, and had been convicted of a felony.

His parole officer wrote that Howard "consumes three to four bottles of hard liquor per week; five cases of beer per week. Drug usage includes peyote during Indian ceremonies only. Cocaine began in 1983. Occasional use. No marks on arms."

Howard's friend Thomas Gutierrez said, "He'd get in fights, he'd get beat up, or he used to get rolled. He would get rolled a lot on the streets. He would pass right out, and people would take his money. He'd be walking downtown, and he would just pass out against a building or something."

In the mid-1980s, Howard found the Native American Indian Center in San Jose and eventually moved in to the halfway house next door. There, Howard lived with eight other end-of-the-line Native alcoholics and started going to Alcoholics Anonymous meetings.

That halfway house is where Howard met Brookey Lee West while Wayne Ike was hiding from her.

Brookey's take on Howard: "When I first met Howard, he looked kind of bad. He was real overweight, and his hair was sort of long. Yet I could see that if he lost some weight and, if he got his hair cut, he would be really good-looking . . . I view life this way – people can be down. They can be sick and they can have a lot of bad things happen, and they can pull themselves back up. That's the way I saw it."

She gave Howard's friends the willies. And they couldn't understand why such a successful woman would want to be with such a loser. They warned him to watch out for an insurance policy.

Howard laughed off his friends' misgivings.

1993 – House In Los Banos, Neighbors On Fir Street, Christine Is Whack

Brookey bought a house on Fir Street in Los Banos in 1993. She brought Christine there to live with her.

Brookey told the neighbors that she had bought the house with a GI loan. She told them that she was a sergeant and that she had flown planes. She also told them the truth, which was that she was a technical writer.

Christine was thin and frail. She had a long braid that hung down to the middle of her back and she always wore a gray sweat suit. Christine made friends with various neighbors. They thought she was lonely and not getting enough nutrition. They found her colorful and interesting but they also thought she was weird and probably insane. Each of them eventually cut themselves off from her.

Christine told the neighbors that she was a strong Cherokee woman who would not take guff from anyone. She talked about being from Ennis and riding the rails with hobos at the age of twelve and pulling a knife on them when they got fresh. She talked about how her granddaughter had been kidnapped from a department store. She gave them bizarre gifts. One was a pair of earrings made out of potatoes.

People who visited Christine saw a room in the house that contained a rack of clothes with the price tags still on them. Some visitors wondered if the reason all those clothes were in the house was because Brookey was running prostitutes. They only had Brookey's say-so that she was a tech writer in Silicon Valley.

Christine would walk into somebody's house unannounced. She and Brookey tried to sell a car to a neighbor for twice what it was worth. Christine brought a neighbor some soup that tasted like pure salt. She claimed she could make love potions.

Christine was proud of her violent history. She bragged about shooting a man in Bakersfield. She said she had been on Death Row until the man came back to life in the morgue. The neighbors knew that was impossible.

Neighbor Laura Parra thought that Brookey looked creepy and might be on drugs.

Everybody could see and hear mother and daughter screaming at each other. They heard Brookey calling her mother a crazy bitch. Brookey told Laura that she didn't like her mother.

Laura: "Brooke said her mom was a lunatic, she was driving her crazy and she didn't want her mom around … she talked about what a pain in the ass her mother was, and her exact words were, 'She's a crazy bitch, and I can't wait to get her out.'"

1994 – Brookey Marries Howard

Howard moved into Brookey's new house early in 1994. Whatever good habits had rubbed off on him at the halfway house were gone. He was drinking again. He drove the neighbors around the bend. He stumbled around drunk out of his mind. He was noisy and rude, he slammed doors, he looked ragged, and the neighbors often heard cursing and bottles breaking.

Some tried to interact with him, but Howard was shy and usually wasted.

A few homes on the street were burgled after Howard moved in, and the neighbors wondered if Howard and Brookey were involved.

His father would not let him get married on the reservation in South Dakota, so Howard and Brookey were married in Reno on April 30. Brookey showed Howard's friends a $20,000 ring that Howard had bought for her, but his friends knew that she had to have bought it for herself.

In their collective opinion, Howard was playing with fire.

Christine and Howard could not stand each other and fought constantly. Brookey bought Christine a van, drove her with her possessions to Santa Clara, parked the van in a parking lot, and told Christine not to come back. According to Leroy, that seemed normal in the relationship dynamic between Brookey and Christine.

Back on Fir Street, Sandy Corona started a Neighborhood Watch program. The only people in the neighborhood not invited to the first meeting on May 21, 1994, were Brookey and Howard. The next day, Sandy found a pile of crushed ice in front of her door. Down the street, she saw Howard toasting her with a bottle of Coke. Sandy was terrified of Howard.

There seemed to be more patrol cars around since Howard had moved in. Sometimes the police visited Brookey's house and the neighbors wondered if it had something to do with the clothes that looked stolen. They wonder if Brookey was a drug dealer. And the husband was always loaded.

Howard's friends continued to worry about him. They knew he didn't fit in where he was living. They didn't trust Brookey.

They visited him in the spring of 1994 and they loved the place. They left within an hour. They didn't like being around Brookey.

Burning The Jaguar

A few weeks later, Howard visited his friends. He told them that Brookey wanted him to burn the Jag for insurance money and he asked his friend Thomas Gutierrez to help him. Gutierrez refused, saying that it would be too easy for the cops to get evidence.

On the night of March 3, 1994, an anonymous caller reported a car fire to 911. When the police showed up to the dirt road, they found a burning 1989 Jaguar – a write-off.

Brookey reported her Jaguar missing about fifty minutes later.

She claimed the car had disappeared while she and her boyfriend were at dinner and a movie. The insurance company paid out $18,897. But they were suspicious about the fire and hired a private investigator to look into it.

Days after the Jag burned, Howard showed up in a Corvette to visit his friends. He told them it was a wedding gift from Brookey. Eventually he admitted to Gutierrez that he had burned the Jag. He said he was nervous because the insurance company was sniffing around.

Howard had just married a woman he hardly knew. Now he was committing crimes for her. Gutierrez again expressed his grave concerns that being involved with Brookey was dangerous for Howard.

The neighbors on Fir Street saw Howard tinkering with the Corvette. When they asked where Brookey's Jag was, they were told that it had been stolen, stripped, and burned.

Dwight Bell was the investigator hired by the insurance company. He later gave authorities a laundry list of suspicious circumstances about the Jag: the car was reported missing *after* it was found burning, everything that is worth stealing from a car was intact, none of the normal causes of car fires were involved, and he had found metal distortion indicative of the involvement of a flammable liquid.

By May 1994, Bell was sure the car had been torched for the insurance money, but he couldn't get in touch with Brookey and he didn't have much actual evidence.

Brookey Shoots Howard

On May 21, 1994, the people of Fir Street saw Howard and Brookey looking very cozy. Mike Stoykovich from across the street saw them hugging and kissing in the garage. Laura and Fermin Parra saw them dancing and embracing in the garage.

At some point, Howard went over to ask Fermin why people didn't like him and Brookey. He wondered if it was Christine's fault. Howard was very drunk. Fermin was polite but went back into his house as soon as he could and told his family to keep away from the St. Johns.

Later that day, the people of Fir Street heard a gunshot. Some thought it was a door slamming and some thought it was a firecracker. They heard yelling. Then they saw Howard stumbling out of the garage covered with blood and screaming, "She shot me!" Someone ran into Parra's house and called 911.

The police officer who responded saw that Howard had a bullet wound on his neck. He heard from Brookey, "I did shoot him, but it was an accident." He heard from Howard, "Bitch, you shot me. I'm going to kill you." Brookey said that Howard was coming at her so she took her .32 out of her purse and pointed it at him, and it "just went off." Brookey said that she called 911.

Howard was taken away in an ambulance and Brookey was taken away in handcuffs.

Brookey told police that they were cleaning the garage when Howard became aggressive. She said there had been a series of domestic disputes before this. During this one, he was obsessing that she might be leaving him. He wanted to have sex on the concrete floor of the garage. She did not want to do that. He threw a table at her. She took the gun out of her purse and it accidentally went off.

She didn't give the police a good reason why her .32 was in her purse while her other guns were locked up. She didn't give them a reason why she had her purse in the garage.

According to Howard's statement to police, Brookey said to him, "I'm setting you up." When the police asked him why she would do such a thing, he told them, "She's a crazy bitch."

Brookey was charged with felony assault with a gun and corporal injury to a spouse. The charges were dropped two weeks later on May 25.

Howard had been flown to a hospital in Modesto. He had a big hole in his neck but no artery had been damaged. The doctors decided to leave the .32 bullet in his left shoulder.

Howard phoned the insurance investigators from his hospital room. He admitted to burning the Jaguar and told them that Brookey had given him a Corvette as payment.

Within a week, Howard was released from the hospital. He visited his old friends. He told Mercado and Gutierrez that Brookey had ambushed him in the garage. She told Howard she was going to kill him because the insurance people were getting suspicious. She said she was going to burn the house down.

Back on Fir Street, Leroy showed up in front of Brookey's house. He talked to neighbor Mike Stoykovich about Brookey's troubles and said how disappointed he was that she had married an Indian. He also said a few racist things about Indians.

He told Stoykovich he had no plans to get her out of jail until she calmed down.

A couple of days later Brookey was out on her own recognizance and Leroy dropped her off on Fir Street.

Brookey told her neighbors that she was afraid of Howard, that she was getting a restraining order and a Rottweiler dog, and that the shooting had been in self-defense because Howard was throwing things at her.

Howard Goes Back To Brookey

It seemed that the Howard and Brookey saga was over. He'd reported her to the insurance people and she'd had a restraining order placed against him. But within a few weeks Brookey told him she would sign the cars and house over to him if he came back. He did.

Howard's friends told him he was crazy. They told him she would kill him. He just had nowhere else to go.

The insurance investigator, Bell, eventually found Howard. He was very drunk, sitting on a bench outside a hospital where he was scheduled to have treatment for his neck wound. While Bell talked to him, Howard chugged a couple of airplane bottles of tequila and chased them with Coke.

He told Bell he had already snorted ½ a gram of meth and drunk six or seven airplane bottles of tequila.

Howard told Bell that he made up the whole story about doing the arson to punish Brookey for shooting him. He gave Bell the original alibi about dinner and a movie. He talked about Brookey's work and his own hernia. He claimed that Brookey had to shoot him because he was slapping her around.

Later he admitted to his friend Tyla Knotchapone that if he'd never met Brookey he wouldn't have a bullet in his neck. "I just want to forget her. She is bad news. I think she's going to kill me," Howard told her.

According to Tyla, "He was in tears, actually. He said, 'I can't believe I have this kind of problem in my life with a woman. This woman is dangerous, Tyla. I don't know how to go about divorcing her. It's like she's got me in a web, and I know the way out, but I'm scared. What could be next? I'm scared to find out.'"

Howard described to Tyla how Brookey abused her mother physically and verbally. After offering him a room at her place, Tyla asked him why he'd gone back to Brookey.

"I'm so stupid," he said. "I don't know why."

Brookey Goes Missing

On June 2, 1994, Brookey ran out into the middle of Fir Street shouting that Howard was threatening to kill her because she had misplaced their wedding photo. The police took her to a coffee shop and she told them she was going to divorce him.

Howard, worried about her, spent the next two days looking for her. He filed a missing persons report on June 4. He thought Brookey had been kidnapped. He pestered the police, but they believed she was voluntarily missing. Howard made some frantic drunken calls to Leroy who assured him that he shouldn't worry about her. Leroy disconnected his phone to get some sleep.

That night, Howard told one of his halfway house friends on the phone that he might have to kill her to get even with her.

Howard Is Shot Dead

Sometime in the twenty-four hours following Howard's last phone conversation, he was shot in the back and his body was dumped near the Tule River in Sequoia National Forest, several hours' drive away from Fir Street.

He wasn't murdered there. He was dumped there like garbage.

Howard's body was discovered in the Forest on June 6, sixteen days after Brookey shot him in the neck and three months after he torched the Jag for her. He had been shot in the back with a .38 handgun.

The police report describes him as a former parolee with eight aliases and fifteen misdemeanors, thirty-five years old, 230 lbs.

It was a sad end to a sad life. People had loved Howard Simon St. John and had hoped that he could turn things around. They will continue to miss him.

When police called Howard's father, Sylvester (no longer disowning him) told them that Howard had been in rehab in San Jose for addiction, that he was married to a woman who lived in Los Banos, and that they had a domestic abuse history.

This led investigators to Brookey.

Brookey had been living in a motel after she left Howard. On June 4, she had picked up Christine at her van in Santa Clara and taken her shopping all day. She went to Silicon Valley to work that night – as a contractor she could work whatever hours she wanted – and the door system showed that she had carded her way in.

Christine and Brookey claimed that Howard had found $3,000 in cash in the house and taken off to Reno to party with friends.

They said that when they returned to the house it was a shambles and that it was full of evidence that people other than Howard had been there that night.

Brookey's story about the whole weekend was full of holes, but investigators were never able to find enough hard evidence to bring charges against her.

Howard's lifestyle offered many other possibilities for why he would have been murdered. Christine herself was a suspect for a while. Investigators believe that, if Brookey did it, both of her parents would have helped her cover it up. The case is officially open to this day.

Thus ended Brookey's third short marriage.

Chloe Sees Leroy's Bad Side

Leroy was diagnosed with brain cancer in 1995 and had a stroke in 1996.

In 1995, Chloe discovered that Leroy had forged her name on twenty-five credit card applications and almost $250,000 in cash advances from those had disappeared. She thought Leroy had given it to Brookey, but Brookey insisted that he had gambled it away.

Chloe also suspected that Brookey had been meddling with Leroy's finances so she would get everything when he died. In early 1996, Brookey told Chloe that she and Leroy had given away his gun collection to pay off thousands of dollars he owed to bookies.

In February 1996, Chloe was looking under Leroy's bed for the titles to six vehicles owned by her and Leroy when Brookey tried to zap her with a stun gun and then tried to hit her with it. Leroy jumped out of his bed and screamed at Chloe that she was a trouble-making bitch. Chloe ran to the parking lot with Brookey chasing her and screaming at her. When Chloe called the police, Brookey drove away.

Leroy told the police that Chloe's story was a lie. Chloe believes that Brookey was trying to kill her and that Leroy was in on it. If Chloe died, Leroy would get $250,000 life insurance which would then go to Brookey when Leroy died. Leroy died two months later.

Thus ended Chloe's marriage with the new and improved Leroy.

Brookey's Fourth Marriage Fizzles: George Burnette

George Burnette, another Native American, looked much like Howard St. John though his black hair hung down to his waist. Burnette and West met in November 1996 at a casino in Las Vegas. Their whirlwind passionate romance began when they spent Thanksgiving Day together.

They were married on January 7, 1997 in Las Vegas.

Within a day of arriving at Brookey's Los Banos house, Brookey told George that she had to go back to Las Vegas to be with her sick mother. The next thing he knew was that Brookey and her car were gone.

He drove to Christine's new apartment in Las Vegas and found that she knew nothing of the marriage. Soon the marriage was annulled. Burnette testified to West's instability at her trial.

Christine Gets A Las Vegas Apartment

In 1997, when Christine was sixty-five, Brookey set her up in a low-rent apartment in Las Vegas. The place was called Orange Door. Christine was still into Jesus and still lying about having Native heritage and still bragging about having been on Death Row for shooting a man. Christine had osteoporosis. Alzheimer's was creeping up on her.

But she became close friends with some of her neighbors. One of them, Alice Wilsey, sixty-six, looked after Christine when Brookey was in California.

Another neighbor, Judy Chang, seventy-four, also enjoyed Christine's company.

Brookey visited often and then moved in with her mother in late 1997. Christine's friends could see that the two loved each other but they also saw the two had bitter arguments.

At some point in 1997, Brookey went AWOL from her job at Hybrid Networks. She had checked herself into a psychiatric hospital. After she got out, she confided more and more in a co-worker, Natalie Hanke.

She told Hanke about a big burglary ring she had once been part of, an exaggeration of her shoplifting escapades with Christine. She told her about Howard's murder and said that she could have done it if someone hadn't beaten her to it. She said her father was a powerful warlock. She talked about how much she hated her mother and what a sociopath and psychopath and financial drain she was. She said that she was going to send her mother to live with Travis who was also a sociopath. They would get along well.

Christine Disappears

Christine was quite sick, bedridden most of the time. The last time Wilsey saw Christine, Brookey was giving her pills, supposedly aspirin. Two days later, Brookey told Chang that Christine had gone to live with Travis in San Jose. This was in February 1998.

West said she had told Christine her only other options were being put in a home or West leaving her there and never coming back. She had driven her to San Jose in the middle of the night, she said.

Christine's friends noticed things that made them suspicious about Brookey's story. They saw some of Christine's possessions in the dumpster. They saw her most prized possessions still in the apartment and believed that Christine would definitely have taken them with her.

On November 11, 1998, Wilsey wrote a letter to the police listing six reasons why she thought Christine had met with foul play. She added that she had witnessed Brookey's violence and mental instability. She outright accused West of killing her mother in a rage. She asked the police to look into Christine's bank account and Social Security checks. She added that she herself was afraid of West.

When she brought the letter to the police, they asked her to come back another day but she never did. She knew that she could be wrong about the entire thing.

Brookey continued to talk about her mother as if she was still a pain in the ass for the whole three years after Christine's friends had last seen her until police discovered Christine's body in the garbage bin.

Natalie Hanke distanced herself from Brookey as she saw more of Brookey's weird side. Brookey continued to rage about her mother. Her Las Vegas apartment was full of weird voodoo-ish things that Brookey claimed were her mother's. The one time Hanke was there, she pretended to be sick just to get away.

Hanke had lunch with Brookey one last time in 1999 during a trip to Las Vegas. Brookey then tried to lure her to the storage locker. Hanke now believes that West was planning to kill her and steal her identity.

Brookey Lee's Luck Comes To An End

In 1985, nobody suspected Brookey or Leroy of any involvement in the shooting of Veramontes' grandmother. In 1985, Brookey and Christine got off with fines and probation for shoplifting. In 1994, it couldn't be proved that Brookey had committed insurance fraud, charges of spousal abuse were dropped, and Howard's murder couldn't be pinned on her. In 1996, she wasn't charged with trying to stun gun her stepmother Chloe.

Then on February 8, 2001, Christine's mostly liquefied body was discovered in the garbage can in the storage unit and identified through dental records.

As the storage locker was in West's name, police got a warrant to search her apartment. They found a key for the storage locker. They found duct tape. They found bank statements showing that $30,000 of Social Security checks in Christine's name had been cashed over the years.

Investigators were not able to catch Brookey at home. But a few days into the investigation, Detective Dave Mesinar saw Brookey's plate number on her truck at a 7-11. Then he saw her inside the store.

On February 8, Brookey was arrested, charged with murder, and taken to Clark County Detention Center without making a statement. She had babbled her face off while being interrogated in the Howard St. John cases.

The next day, she was interviewed by a TV news anchor and said that her mother had died of natural causes and she had put her in the trash bin rather than report the death. This made things easier for Mesinar, because he would not have to look for other suspects.

West's involvement was further confirmed when a single print of hers was found on the plastic that sealed the trash can.

The Investigation

Mesinar received information from Daniel Haynes, an investigator in Howard's murder case, and found out that there had been a plastic bag partially on Howard's face when his body was found.

Haynes gave Mesinar a lot of other information about Brookey's life and background. Mesinar concluded that she was certainly capable of killing.

Investigators and the prosecutor Frank Coumou believed Brookey had killed her mother for the money, out of hatred, and because commuting between Las Vegas and San Jose was inconvenient.

Mesinar and his team dug in and interviewed all the people who had known Brookey and Christine. They spent weeks looking for Brookey's brother Travis but, like Haynes before them, they couldn't find him alive or dead. They did find out that around the time Travis was last seen alive Brookey had written to Social Security to have Travis' checks deposited into an account that she had access to.

Mesinar realized that, if Brookey had killed her mother, her husband, and her brother, she was a serial killer. (It has never been proved that West killed St. John and it has never been proved that Travis Lee Smith is dead.)

The medical examiner wasn't able to confirm that Christine was murdered. Her body was too decomposed. But the pathologists were able to prove murder through maggot evidence.

If Christine had been found dead and then put in the bin, as Brookey claimed, the maggots would have been from blowflies. Blowflies find their way to a corpse almost instantly. But the maggots were from coffin flies not blowflies, indicating that Christine's body had been sealed into the bin before blowflies had a chance to find her body.

Investigators thought it was likely that Christine was still alive when she was sealed in the bin. The lack of blowflies certainly proved pre-meditation.

Trial & Conviction

West pleaded not guilty at a preliminary hearing. The trial began on July 6, 2001.

Brookey's defense continued to be that her mother had a lot of medical problems and died of natural causes. Evidence about Christine's medical history was presented at trial. Brookey discovered Christine's body and put her in the bin so she wouldn't have to deal with police. She was still a suspect in Howard's murder and wanted no involvement with them in relation to yet another death.

She didn't deny spending her mother's checks and the prosecution presented evidence that somebody, probably Brookey, had been cashing them.

The prosecution argued that the motives were hatred and money. After reading Brookey's books from the storage locker, Coumou developed a theory involving Satanism that dovetailed with the way Christine's body had been disposed and the plastic bag on her face. But he left that theory out of the trial, worried about future appeals.

The prosecution tore apart the "living with Travis" story because he'd been homeless and then missing for years. If the jury believed that Christine had been living with Travis for some of the past three years, it would shoot down the idea that Brookey had Christine in the storage locker and was cashing her checks the entire time.

Travis had last been seen in 1993. His last known mailing address was the Los Banos house that Brookey and Christine had lived in. His disability checks were cut off in 1999 when administrators couldn't get in touch with him. His driver's license had been expired for ages.

The judge did not allow the prosecution to hint that Travis might be dead, though prosecutors suspected that Brookey had killed him for his checks.

A slew of witnesses, including West's fourth husband and Natalie Hanke, testified about West's personality.

Closing arguments took place on July 18. It took the jury two hours to find Brookey Lee West guilty of first degree murder. The primary reasons for the conviction were the plastic bag around Christine's face and the maggots being the wrong kind of maggots.

Sentence

In September 1994, Judge Mosley sentenced Brookey Lee West to life without parole. He firmly believed that

Christine had been deliberately suffocated with the plastic bag.

"We've heard two possible explanations. One is that it was a shroud . . . in deference to the decedent's status. And, of course, we've heard the other suggestion – that it was, in essence, what killed her by virtue of suffocating.

"I have to tell you, Ms. West, that the latter is more likely in my view. She was overpowered, this item placed around her face, tied tightly, and she was placed into this garbage container, presumably to suffocate her . . ."

Mosely finished with, "While I think everyone would agree putting someone's mother in a garbage can to bury her is bizarre, placing her in there conscious to suffocate her is not only bizarre – it's criminal. You are sentenced to life without the possibility of parole. That's all."

Appeals

Brookey unsuccessfully appealed her conviction in 2003. Her side argued that a natural death due to medical issues had not been disproved. The appeal Justices said that the circumstances "clearly created a reasonable inference of Smith's death by criminal agency."

The Justices also rejected her lawyer's argument that Judge Mosley had erred in admitting photographs of the victim. They opined that gruesome photos have to be allowed if they help with "ascertaining the truth" and these photos helped jurors to see the importance of the plastic bag.

In 2004, Brookey had hopes of a new trial when it was discovered that a man using her brother's name and Social

Security number had been to the Santa Clara Medical Center in San Jose. Investigators weren't able to track this person down. There is a possibility that this person, Travis or not, moved on to Florida. Nobody ever found him.

Finding Travis wouldn't have helped Brookey though. Her trial jury had heard a recording of her saying, "No one knows where he is and no one has seen him in years," which flew in the face of her claim that Christine had been living with him.

In appealing her sentence in 2006, her lawyer argued that she would have been handed a lighter sentence if Veramontes' evidence about being intimidated with Satanic threats had not been presented.

The Supreme Court of Nevada ruled that she was "not sentenced by virtue of some mistreatment that [she] foisted upon Mr. Veramontes." The judge "felt the evidence was overwhelming as to [her] guilt."

Prison

Brookey Lee West is serving her sentence in the Florence McClure Women's Correctional Center near Las Vegas. She is a model prisoner. She leads a Bible study class. She teaches art. She helps raise awareness and money to help Nevada's wild horses.

She denies involvement in any crimes except shoplifting. She does admit that Leroy sent the threatening letter to her daughter's father. She says that in 1999 she was bringing her mother back from Travis to Las Vegas and her mother died in a hotel room on the way.

In 2008 she was sending product to a man who sells murderabilia online. He sold some of her art and some t-shirts that she had worn and signed. He didn't find a buyer for her fingernail clippings at $19.95.

In July 2012 Brookey attempted a prison break. She changed her appearance and tried to walk out while the inmates were heading to breakfast. Staff recognized her standing near a security gate, right next to the main exit/entrance.

Judge Donald Mosley said in a TV interview: "It was one of the most bizarre trials I've had in my now thirty years on the bench . . . I never saw one iota of remorse . . . I think, all things considered, Brookey West got exactly what she deserved."